Ezra–Nehemiah

INTERPRETATION
A Bible Commentary for Teaching and Preaching

INTERPRETATION
A BIBLE COMMENTARY FOR TEACHING AND PREACHING

James Luther Mays, *Editor*
Patrick D. Miller, Jr., *Old Testament Editor*
Paul J. Achtemeier, *New Testament Editor*

MARK A. THRONTVEIT

Ezra-Nehemiah

INTERPRETATION

A Bible Commentary
for Teaching and Preaching

John Knox Press
LOUISVILLE

Library of Congress Cataloging-in-Publication Data

Throntveit, Mark A., 1949–
   Ezra-Nehemiah / Mark A. Throntveit.
      p.   cm. — (Interpretation, a Bible commentary for teaching and preaching)
   Includes bibliographical references.
   ISBN 0-8042-3111-7

   1. Bible. O.T. Ezra—Commentaries. 2. Bible. O.T. Nehemiah—Commentaries. I. Title. II. Series.
BS1355.3.T47 1991
222′.707—dc20   91-32970

To the memory of my mother,

Louise Bilstad Throntveit

SERIES PREFACE

This series of commentaries offers an interpretation of the books of the Bible. It is designed to meet the need of students, teachers, ministers, and priests for a contemporary expository commentary. These volumes will not replace the historical critical commentary or homiletical aids to preaching. The purpose of this series is rather to provide a third kind of resource, a commentary which presents the integrated result of historical and theological work with the biblical text.

An interpretation in the full sense of the term involves a text, an interpreter, and someone for whom the interpretation is made. Here, the text is what stands written in the Bible in its full identity as literature from the time of "the prophets and apostles," the literature which is read to inform, inspire, and guide the life of faith. The interpreters are scholars who seek to create an interpretation which is both faithful to the text and useful to the church. The series is written for those who teach, preach, and study the Bible in the community of faith.

The comment generally takes the form of expository essays. It is planned and written in the light of the needs and questions which arise in the use of the Bible as Holy Scripture. The insights and results of contemporary scholarly research are used for the sake of the exposition. The commentators write as exegetes and theologians. The task which they undertake is both to deal with what the texts say and to discern their meaning for faith and life. The exposition is the unified work of one interpreter.

The text on which the comment is based is the Revised Standard Version of the Bible and, since its appearance, the New Revised Standard Version. The general availability of these translations makes the printing of a text in the commentary unnecessary. The commentators have also had other current versions in view as they worked and refer to their readings where it is helpful. The text is divided into sections appropriate to the particular book; comment deals with passages as a whole, rather than proceeding word by word, or verse by verse.

Writers have planned their volumes in light of the requirements set by the exposition of the book assigned to them. Biblical books differ in character, content, and arrangement. They also differ in the way they have been and are used in the liturgy, thought, and devotion of the church. The distinctiveness and use of particular books have been taken into account in decisions about the approach, emphasis, and use of space in the commentaries. The goal has been to allow writers to develop the format which provides for the best presentation of their interpretation.

The result, writers and editors hope, is a commentary which both explains and applies, an interpretation which deals with both the meaning and the significance of biblical texts. Each commentary reflects, of course, the writer's own approach and perception of the church and world. It could and should not be otherwise. Every interpretation of any kind is individual in that sense; it is one reading of the text. But all who work at the interpretation of Scripture in the church need the help and stimulation of a colleague's reading and understanding of the text. If these volumes serve and encourage interpretation in that way, their preparation and publication will realize their purpose.

The Editors

ACKNOWLEDGMENTS

The completion of this manuscript elicits expressions of gratitude for those who have assisted in its production. I am grateful to the administration and Board of Directors of Luther Northwestern Theological Seminary for their generous sabbatical program, a program enhanced by the support of Aid Association for Lutherans and Lutheran Brotherhood. This support made possible a sabbatical year in Cambridge, England, where the groundwork for the commentary was laid. While I was in England, the resources of Tyndale House provided a supportive and challenging environment. My family and I also enjoyed the warm hospitality of Professors Ronald Clements, R. N. Whybray, John Emerton, and especially Hugh Williamson, whose example and expertise I treasure as much as his friendship.

My interest in the Persian period began in graduate school with an investigation of the work of the Chronicler. It has continued through participation in the Chronicles–Ezra–Nehemiah Group of the Society of Biblical Literature. Presentations by and discussions with Ralph Klein, Tamara Eskenazi, Ray Dillard, Joseph Blenkinsopp, and other colleagues have deepened my appreciation of the complexity of this puzzling period.

I am grateful to Professors James Luther Mays and Patrick D. Miller, Jr., for inviting me to contribute to the series. Their patient support and critique at all stages of the manuscript were invaluable.

Student response, arising out of a doctoral seminar in Ezra–Nehemiah at Luther Northwestern Seminary, further shaped and refined many of the positions taken in the commentary. My teaching assistant, Peter Lockwood, contributed much needed help in the final revisions.

Finally, I would like to express my love for Karol, Trygve, and Trevor, whose love and support continue to sustain and refresh me.

Mark A. Throntveit

CONTENTS

INTERPRETATION

Introduction

The editorial policy defined for this series, which stresses the integration of exegesis and hermeneutical reflection into one readable expository essay without a separate movement through the various exegetical steps, promises closer articulation of the text's significance for the life of faith and its relation to the church. The emphasis upon sections of text that are used in teaching and preaching, rather than individual verses and words, indicates its commitment to the interrelatedness and message of biblical books as a whole.

History or Story? On Reading Ezra–Nehemiah

Ezra–Nehemiah, however, presents particular challenges with regard to this editorial policy. While we rarely hear the *story* of Ezra–Nehemiah proclaimed from the pulpit, as our primary source for the *history* of the restoration these books have enjoyed considerable scholarly attention. Yet it is precisely in the area of history that Ezra–Nehemiah is commonly regarded as bristling with problems: Who came first, Ezra or Nehemiah? When did Ezra make his journey to Jerusalem? How many journeys did he, in fact, make? Under which Artaxerxes did he go? Were Ezra and Nehemiah contemporaries? If so, how is it that they never refer to each other or to the other's work? Though these questions have exercised commentators and historians for generations, they are still vigorously debated without consensus.

This is especially evident in the vexing relationship between Ezra and Nehemiah. The traditional view holds that Ezra preceded Nehemiah, arriving from Babylon in "the seventh year of King Artaxerxes" (Ezra 7:7–8). If this ruler was Artaxerxes I (465–424 B.C.), this would be 458 B.C. Nehemiah's return, which is reasonably secure, occurred some thirteen years later in 445 B.C.

Many scholars, however, question this sequence on the basis of several apparent discrepancies and place Ezra's return after Nehemiah, in 398 B.C., maintaining that the ruler in question was Artaxerxes II (404–360 B.C.).

Other scholars insist that a 428 B.C. date best explains the evidence. This dating depends on textual emendation of Ezra 7:7–8, from "the seventh year" to the *"thirty*-seventh year" on the basis of haplography. The discussion of this matter is extremely complex. While the 398 B.C.E. date earlier enjoyed a modest consensus, recent works tend to favor the traditional dating (see Kidner, pp. 146–158).

In the past scholars such as C. C. Torrey and W. Rudolph, recognizing these historical problems in the narrative, especially the problems that arise from the interleaving of the Ezra material (Ezra 7—10; Nehemiah 8—10) with that of Nehemiah (Nehemiah 1—7, 11—13), attempted to resolve them by positing an originally tripartite work structured by the activities of the three great leaders of the postexilic period. Zerubbabel was assigned the task of rebuilding the temple, Ezra reinstituted the law, and Nehemiah rebuilt the walls of Jerusalem. All three successfully completed their missions despite opposition, and for all three the completion of their tasks was marked by a great assembly. Rearrangement of the text to its "original" order revealed the following schematic outline:

A. Zerubbabel (538–515 B.C.)
1. Reconstruction of the temple (Ezra 1:1—6:15)
2. Assembly for celebration and Passover (Ezra 6:16–22)
B. Ezra (458–457 B.C.)
1. Reinstitution of the Law (Ezra 7—8, Nehemiah 7:73b—8:18, Ezra 9—10)
2. Assembly for fasting and confession (Nehemiah 9—10)
C. Nehemiah (446–433 B.C.)
1. Reconstruction of the walls and repopulating of Jerusalem (Nehemiah 1:1—7:73a, 11:1—12:26)
2. Assembly and dedication (Nehemiah 12:27—13:3)
Appendix: Cultic reforms of Nehemiah (Nehemiah 13:4–31)

Despite the problems involved with such massive rearrangement of the text, various refinements of this position have dominated the literature until quite recently. Currently, however, concern for the final form of biblical material is growing as scholars become increasingly frustrated with the results of a more diachronic approach. (For a helpful review the interested

2

reader is referred to the recent commentaries of Williamson, Blenkinsopp, and Clines.)

One of the reasons for the apparently insoluble nature of these historical problems lies in the questionable presupposition that the material has been ordered in accordance with historical or chronological criteria. But as R. J. Coggins says:

> For him [the Chronicler] the maxim, "first things first" meant, not as it might for us, a chronological order, but an order of importance. The temple must come first, then the purifying of the community, then the building of the outer walls of the city, and so finally all could reach a grand climax in the reading of the law (p. 107).

A theological reading of the material that takes account of its character as narrative, as story, and concentrates on the final form of the text, would obviate the need to answer several of the preceding historical questions.

The Plan of the Commentary

This commentary, then, will usually avoid rearrangements of the text. With the exception of Nehemiah 5, which is out of place in terms of both a historical and a literary reading of the text, the commentary will seek to understand the narrative as it has been received.

This commentary will also usually avoid an overly historical approach to the text that seeks to determine "what really happened." As is becoming clear, ancient historians have very little, if any, interest in such matters. Their concern was rather to

> press forward paradigms, privileged symbols, and patterns, through which their readers might meaningfully, indeed consolingly, bring the past down into their present and launch themselves successfully into the future. The assumption of the biblical historians is that who or what Israel is may be found in what Israel has been, and that the core of what Israel has been lies in the intrigue and challenge of its bond with the divine mystery (Carmody, Carmody, and Cohn, p. 413).

One such paradigm encountered in these books depicts the crucial theological moments of the restoration as three parallel returns: under Zerubbabel (Ezra 1—6), Ezra (Ezra 7—10), and Nehemiah (Neh. 1:1—7:3), each of which resulted in a different project of reconstruction, namely, the temple, the community, and the walls. All three share a progression:

3

1. initial return under the divinely prompted authorization of the Persian crown, followed by
2. nearly constant opposition to reconstruction, and
3. the overcoming of the opposition with divine aid.

This paradigm, with its dual emphasis upon return and reconstruction, suggests a structure for Part One of the commentary: "Return and Reconstruction" (Ezra 1:1—Neh. 7:3). The overriding concern of this initial section, as revealed in each of the three returns and building projects, is to demonstrate the returned community's continuity with the past. This concern perhaps best explains the several allusions to the exodus that pepper the narrative.

If Part One links the three returns and reconstruction projects in an attempt to establish the community's continuity with the past, Part Two of the commentary, "Renewal and Reform" (Neh. 7:4—12:43), sees these three areas of community concern in dire need of renewal and reform if the community is to have any share in the future. This concern perhaps best explains why the dedication of the walls is delayed in the narrative until Nehemiah 12:27ff., after the reforms have had their effect in the renewal of the people and their institutions.

As satisfying as this concern for past and future may be, the text will not allow us to end on the optimistic note of the joyous dedication. In what is best regarded as a coda, Nehemiah 12:44—13:31 (5:1-19), refuses to relieve the tension between reform and subsequent relapse that has characterized the work as a whole and invites the reader to contemplate the continuing need for present commitment in the life of faith.

Literary Conventions

In the development of this plan, the commentary generally has concerned itself with the exposition of rather large pericopes. This has resulted from careful observation of the literary markers present in the surface structure of the text itself. Three basic conventions dominate the literary architecture: concentricity, parallel panels, and repetitive resumptions.

Concentricity. In concentric arrangements the members of the second half of a bicolon, sentence, or other literary unit echo, repeat, or recall the members of the first half in inverted order, in the form AB . . . B'A'. If there are only four members, the concentric arrangement is properly a "chiasmus," named

4

after the physical similarity to the Greek letter X *(chi)* when the members are arranged as follows:

$$A \diagdown B$$
$$B' \diagup \diagdown A'$$

Of the numerous instances of this construction in both Old and New Testaments, Jesus' words in Mark 2:27 will serve as a simple illustration:

A   *The sabbath*
  B   was made for *humankind,*
  B'   and not *humankind*
A'   for *the sabbath*

When more than two pairs of members occur, that is, when there is a series of three or more pairings, the structure is properly a "concentric arrangement" in the form ABC . . . C'B'A'. The offensive imprecation at the heart of Psalm 58, in its Hebrew word order, is a clear example:

A   *O God*
  B   *break*
    C   their *teeth* in their mouth
    C'   the *fangs* of the lions
  B'   *break out*
A'   *O Lord*
          (v.7, RSV [v.6, NRSV])

Frequently, a central member (X) will function as a "hinge," or turning point, in the unit: ABC . . . X . . . C'B'A'. Occasionally—but not always!—this central member, thus set in rhetorical exposure, contains the main point of the author. Numbers 15:35–36, again following the word order of the original, displays the hingelike, pivoting function of a central, unparalleled member:

A   Then *the Lord* said to *Moses,*
  B   "The man shall be put *to death;*
    C   they shall *stone him with stones,*
      D   *all the congregation, outside the camp."*
        X   THEN THEY BROUGHT HIM OUT,
      D'   *all the congregation, outside the camp,*
    C'   and *stoned him with stones*
  B'   *to death*
A'   as *the Lord* commanded *Moses.*

5

In this configuration, A-D relates God's command, while D'-A' relates its (literal!) "execution," the congregation's step-by-step carrying out of the command, after the turning point (X).

As illustrated in the commentary, concentricity is the primary structural device employed in Ezra–Nehemiah, appearing at every level of the text. In Ezra not only are the three major units (chapters 1—6, 7—8, and 9—10) so structured but the majority of their subunits (1:7–11, 4:8–23, 5:1—6:22; 7:1b–5, 7:11–26; 9:1—10:1a, 10:1b–44) are as well.

In Nehemiah a similar situation exists. In addition to the extensive concentric arrangement of the so-called "Nehemiah Memoir" (Neh. 1:1b—7:3, with concentrically arranged subunits and sections: 1:1b—2:20, 1:5–11a, 2:11–16, 2:17–20; 3:1—4:23, 4:7–23; 6:1—7:3), the Covenant Renewal passage (7:73b—10:39), which itself is structured according to the principle of parallel panels (see below), the Dedication Service (12: 27–43), and the later reforms of Nehemiah (12:44—13:13) employ concentric arrangements to a great extent (8:13–18, 9:5b–37, 9:38—10:39; 12:27–31, 37–40, 43; 12:44—13:13).

Concentricity's principal value, at least in this portion of Scripture, lies in helping the reader to determine the extent of literary units, as well as revealing the inner logic of the units so identified. Biblical narratives in general, and Old Testament narratives in particular, are frequently characterized as monotonous and repetitious by those who consciously or unconsciously apply the stylistic conventions of a language with a varied vocabulary and rich in synonyms, such as English, to Hebrew. But if the repetitions function structurally rather than stylistically, this negative, ethnocentric judgment loses its force. More importantly, the structural significance of the repetitions can be utilized in keeping with their intended function.

Parallel Panels. On occasion, particularly where the temporal flow of a unit would be obscured by a concentric ordering of the material, parallel panels, in the form Panel I ABCD . . . Panel II A'B'C'D', where the echoes and/or repetitions are not inverted but follow the same sequence, serve to structure the unit. As is the case with the more usual concentric arrangement, this structural device enhances the juxtaposition of similar material and helps in the proper delimitation of literary units. Paul uses this device in I Corinthians 3:6–7 to good effect:

Panel I
  A   I *planted,*
    B   Apollos *watered,*
      C but *God gave the growth* (v. 6).

Panel II
  A' So neither the one who *plants*
    B' nor the one who *waters* is anything,
      C' but only *God who gives the growth* (v. 7).

In Ezra–Nehemiah the most significant use of parallel panels as a structuring device occurs in Nehemiah 7:73b—10:39, where each of the three scenes that constitute the narrative (7:73b—8:12; 8:13-18; 9:1—10:39) follows the same sequence:

	Scene I *7:73b—8:12*	Scene II *8:13-18*	Scene III *9:1—10:39*
A time reference	7:73b	A' 8:13a	A" 9:1a
B assembly	8:1-2	B' 8:13b	B" 9:1b-2
C encounter with Law	8:3-6	C' 8:13c	C" 9:3
D application	8:7-11	D' 8:14-15	D" 9:4-37
E response	8:12	E' 8:16-18	E" 9:38-10:39

As the commentary will make clear, we are thus encouraged to read Nehemiah 7:73b—10:39 as a unit that culminates in the people's *response* to the law and focuses our attention on the renewal of the congregation rather than on Ezra's reading of the law, as is usually the case.

Other significant instances of parallel panels in Ezra–Nehemiah include:

1. Nehemiah 6:1-9 and 6:10-14, in which the first two of three schemes designed to intimidate Nehemiah share the same four-stage progression;

2. Nehemiah 12:32-36 and 12:38-42, which present the two thanksgiving processionals that march around the rebuilt walls at the dedication service in parallel fashion;

3. Nehemiah 13:15-22 and 13:23-29, which parallel Nehemiah's reforming activity after his second return; and

4. Part One of the entire work (Ezra 1:1—Neh. 7:3), which parallels the three returns from Babylon under Zerubbabel, Ezra, and Nehemiah, as outlined above. The proposal of Torrey,

followed by many others, that Nehemiah 8—10 originally followed either Ezra 8 or Ezra 10 and should be so repositioned, however plausible this may be on historical grounds, fails to take adequate account of the clear structuring of the received text.

The schematic arrangement of these and other parallel panels, as well as the concentric arrangements listed above, can be found in the discussion of these passages in the commentary.

Repetitive Resumption. Of less overall significance—but of crucial importance for the interpretation of Ezra 4:6–24—is the literary convention of repetitive resumption first observed in these books by S. Talmon (*IDBSup,* p. 322). In repetitive resumptions the thread of an interrupted narrative is picked up by repeating the last clause prior to the interruption, though generally with some textual variation, thus indicating the digressionary character of the interruption.

Talmon discerns four such instances in the narrative of Ezra–Nehemiah:

1. Ezra 4:6–24 digresses from the summary notation of Ezra 4:4–5, which is picked up again in 4:24b, "the reign of King Darius of Persia."

2. Ezra 6:19–22a is shown to be digressionary by 6:16b's mention of the joy the people experienced at the completion of the temple in 6:22b.

3. Ezra 2:2–69, the long list of returnees, intrudes between the similarly worded 2:1b and 2:70.

4. Nehemiah 7:73b—10:39, depicted as a covenant renewal, breaks the continuity of Nehemiah 7:4–5 and 11:1, which both speak of the tithing of the people as a means of repopulating Jerusalem.

The widespread use of these literary conventions in biblical narrative has been increasingly recognized in the guild. To the growing list of documentation, Jacob Milgrom's clear, concise discussion of these matters in the introduction to his JPS Torah Commentary on *Numbers* (1990), should now be added. It is hoped that this kind of reading will open up new lines of interpretation and understanding in these books.

The Question of Authorship

8

For the past twenty years, the question of the common authorship of Chronicles, Ezra, and Nehemiah has been vigorously debated. In a number of books and articles Sarah Japhet and H. G. M. Williamson have led the way in challenging the widely held view that these books flow from a common source, a view that rests on four basic arguments:

1. The presence of the first verses of Ezra at the end of Chronicles
2. The evidence of 1 Esdras, which begins with II Chronicles 35—36 and continues through Ezra
3. Linguistic similarities between Chronicles and Ezra–Nehemiah
4. The similarity of theological conception in both works

While Japhet and Williamson have provided strong arguments against the ability of the first three of the above to prove common authorship, they have not been able to show separate authorship on these grounds (Throntveit, "Linguistic Analysis"). However, research on the fourth point—the supposed similarity of theological conception—is more conclusive. Among the differences now perceived are the following:

1. The Chronicler's emphasis on David and the Davidic Covenant, so prominent in Chronicles, is totally lacking in Ezra–Nehemiah.
2. Similarly, the exodus traditions prominent in Ezra–Nehemiah are virtually ignored by Chronicles.
3. Ezra–Nehemiah's abhorrence of marriages with foreigners is difficult to explain in light of the tolerant attitude expressed toward Solomon's mixed marriages in Chronicles.
4. The Chronicler's frequent use of immediate retribution as a theological lodestone is absent in Ezra–Nehemiah.

The recent commentaries of A. H. J. Gunneweg and J. Blenkinsopp, however, show that the debate is far from over. While I am among those who deny the common authorship of Chronicles and Ezra–Nehemiah, I am convinced that one's opinions in this matter color the interpretation of Chronicles to a far greater extent than they do that of Ezra–Nehemiah. For this reason, then, the exposition will only rarely make use of material from Chronicles as it seeks to explain the message of Ezra–Nehemiah as a discreet canonical entity.

Following Williamson (*Ezra, Nehemiah,* pp. xxxii–xxxvi), this commentary sees three basic stages in the literary history of Ezra–Nehemiah: (1) the composition of the various primary

9

sources, all more or less contemporary with the events they relate; (2) the composition of the so-called "Ezra Memoir" and "Nehemiah Memoir," as well as other material, to form Ezra 7:1—Nehemiah 11:20; 12:27—13:31 about 400 B.C. (the lists contained in Neh. 11:21—12:26 were added separately); and (3) the later composition and addition of Ezra 1—6, as the final redactor's introduction to the whole, about 300 B.C.

Setting and Message

Ezra–Nehemiah provides an excellent example of the way in which Israel retold old stories to address new situations in the life of God's people. The disastrous events of 587 B.C., which included the destruction of the temple, the end of the Davidic monarchy and Israel as a political entity, not to mention the deportation of the fruit and flower of the population to exile in Babylon, had necessitated a radical reassessment of Israel's identity and relationship to God. How should they understand what had happened to them? Had God sent them into exile, or had the gods of Babylon been victorious? Were they still the chosen people, or had God abandoned them? What had gone wrong? Was God able to deliver them? Was God willing to deliver them? Would God remember the promises to Abraham and David?

The answers to these questions had been largely negative. The tremendous theological responses engendered by the exile, though varied and arising out of differing perspectives within the community, were united in interpreting these events as God's judgment on an unrepentant Israel in fulfillment of the prophetic warnings and resulting in a clean break with the past. As Second Isaiah reports:

> Who gave up Jacob to the spoiler,
>   and Israel to the robbers?
> Was it not the LORD, against whom we have sinned,
>   in whose ways they would not walk,
>   and whose law they would not obey?
>
> (Isa. 42:24)
>
> But Zion said, "The LORD has forsaken me,
>   my Lord has forgotten me."
>
> (Isa. 49:14)

10

Toward the end of this period, however, Israel began to see that the judgment of exile, though necessary and justified, was not God's final word. Hope that the old promises to Abraham and David might yet be realized was rekindled through the preaching of Second Isaiah and the recasting of tradition by the priests.

Ezra 1—6, coming from the pen of the final compiler of Ezra–Nehemiah early in the Hellenistic period (about 300 B.C.) as an introduction to the earlier combination of the Ezra and Nehemiah records (see H. G. M. Williamson, "The Composition of Ezra i–vi," *JTS* 34:1–30 [1983]), addresses a community that had experienced the initial fulfillment of that hope. This new situation in the life of God's people demanded a message differing from both the earlier recognition of judgment and Second Isaiah's proclamation of hope. A word of encouragement was needed by a community involved in the process of reconstruction, a community that desperately needed to hear of its ties with the past. Though the Israel that emerged from the crucible of exile was not the same as the nation that had gone before, the institutions that were slowly developing sought to mediate the same promise and heritage that had nurtured Israel of old. The validity of those institutions as vehicles for transmitting the promise, and above all the assurance of continuity with the past and sense of identity that their legitimacy provided, were what these people most needed to hear. That need was met by retelling the story of the return, a story to which we now turn.

PART ONE

Return and Reconstruction

EZRA 1:1—NEHEMIAH 7:3

Ezra–Nehemiah begins with an extended treatment of the formative days of the restoration period. In the perspective of these books, however, theology and not chronology forms the basis of the presentation. In its present form, the salient theological moments of the restoration period coincide with three parallel returns spanning nearly a century and separated by significant chronological gaps:

1. Sheshbazzar/Zerubbabel (538 B.C.; Ezra 1—6);
2. Ezra (458 B.C.; Ezra 7—10);
3. Nehemiah (445 B.C.; Nehemiah 1:1—7:3).

Each of these three returns culminates in a different project of reconstruction: respectively, the temple, the community, and the walls of Jerusalem. In addition, all three share a common progression in which an initial return under the divinely prompted authorization of the Persian crown (Ezra 1:1; 6:22; 7:6, 27f.; Neh. 1:11; 2:4, 8) is followed by nearly constant opposition to the reconstruction project and the overcoming of the opposition with God's help.

Each of the three returns that structure this first part of Ezra–Nehemiah has been carefully crafted to proclaim that the postexilic community stands in strict continuity with its preexilic ancestors in an attempt to assure the reader that one can live a life of faith even when one is subjected to foreign rule.

Return Under Zerubbabel
and Reconstruction of Temple

EZRA 1—6

A number of earlier sources—the proclamation of Cyrus that enabled the return (1:2–4), the list of temple vessels (1:9–11a), the long list of those who had returned with Zerubbabel (2:1–67), two letters summarized in 4:6 and 7, and two additional sets of Aramaic correspondence between the community's opponents (4:8–16; 5:6–17) and the Persian throne (4:17–22; 6:3–12) the latter including the official transcript of Cyrus's proclamation in verses 3–5—are skillfully woven into the fabric of a narrative designed to accentuate the continuity between the present community and the past. This is done in a number of ways, the investigation of which will order the exposition.

Ezra 1—2
Continuity with the Past

That It Might Be Accomplished (1:1–4)

Something new had happened! In the past, God had frequently made use of foreign nations through the agency of their kings, but God's purpose had always been to chastise Israel. The nations had become the rods of divine wrath (e.g., Isa. 5:26–30; 7:18–19; 10:5; Hos. 10:10; Amos 6:14; I Chron. 5:26; II Chron. 21:16). The Chronicler's final example of this activity records the devastation that resulted in the Babylonian exile:

> Therefore he [God] brought up against them the king of the Chaldeans, who killed their youths with the sword in the house of their sanctuary, and had no compassion on young man or young woman, the aged or the feeble; he [God] gave them all into his [the king's] hand (II Chron. 36:17).

13

But now, when he "stirred up the spirit of King Cyrus of Persia" (1:1) with the positive intention of redemption that Israel might return to the land, God's use of the nations encompassed a new purpose.

Seen against the backdrop of ancient history, there is little to commend the audacity of this claim. As the long inscription known to us from the Cyrus Cylinder makes plain, the Persian throne returned *all* the exiled communities in Babylon without distinction and covered the initial costs of the rebuilding of their sanctuaries, that "all gods which I have brought to their cities pray daily to Bel and Nabu for my length of days." The motivation, at least in Cyrus's opinion, was political. Whereas the Babylonians had attempted to quash rebellion and thereby solidify their position by deporting potential threats to their security, Cyrus and the Persians felt that as a matter of policy it was preferable to provide the subject peoples of the empire with a measure of self-determination and religious autonomy in the hope that this enlightened approach would instill feelings of loyalty.

Nevertheless, the audacious claim of the text remains. It was God who "stirred" Cyrus to make his monumental proclamation. The reason for God's activity in this regard is also given: "that the word of the LORD by the mouth of Jeremiah might be accomplished." The specific prophecy referred to is Jeremiah 29:10:

> For thus says the LORD: Only when Babylon's seventy years are completed will I visit you, and I will fulfill to you my promise and bring you back to this place.

Attempts to account for the seventy-year period have tended to obscure the emphasis on the return. Possibly the period of Jehoiakim's exile (II Chron. 36:6) is to be included along with the primary period following the fall of Jerusalem in 587. A fairly exact correspondence would cover the period between the destruction of the temple in 587 and its completed restoration in 515 (cf. Zech. 1:12; 7:5). Be that as it may, the text is concerned with the return itself as the primary fulfillment of Jeremiah's vision. As if to cement this emphasis, Ezra 1:1 conflates material from Second Isaiah that refers to God's stirring up of Cyrus to overthrow Babylon and restore Israel in its presentation (41:2; 44:28; 45:1, 13; but notice this emphasis in Jer. 51:1 as well).

The importance of this textual claim lies in its intended

14

effect upon the community. By insisting that the return be interpreted as the activity of the same God who had previously raised up Israel's enemies for judgment, the overriding concern for continuity is preserved. The questions of the community regarding their place in God's plan and God's disposition toward them were decisively answered in such a way that restoration was enabled and encouraged. All the might and power of the ancient world was under the control of their God, and their God had chosen to place it at their disposal.

Thus, these few verses proclaim nothing less than the announcement of God's gracious activity in fulfillment of the hopes and promises the great prophets of the exile had used to ease the pain of God's judgment. They summon the restoration community to regard themselves as Israel reborn, recalled from the grave of doubt and despair to walk in the newness of this latest recreation of God's people. God had not forgotten them. God had not been defeated by the gods of Babylon. God had been faithful to the promises all along. Even in the chastisement of the people during the seventy years of exile, divine grace is attested in God's refusal to give them over to death. God was with them, in their midst, and at their head, leading them on to a second chance, a new opportunity to affirm their place in the great plan of redemption.

A Second Exodus (1:5–11)

Just as God had "stirred up the spirit of King Cyrus of Persia so that he sent a herald," which enabled the return from Babylon (1:1), so now the people's faithful response to that proclamation came from "everyone whose spirit God had stirred . . . to go up" (1:5). In reading these books of the postexilic restoration, so frequently characterized by an emphasis on Law, obedience, and narrow perspective, it is crucial to see that they begin with twin statements that affirm the gracious prompting of God as the motivational force behind both aspects of the return. The pattern will continue throughout the narrative. The second major section of the story, Ezra 7—10, will begin with God's prompting of the Persian king to act benevolently toward Israel by granting Ezra "all that he asked, for the hand of the LORD his God was upon him" (7:6). Similarly, the third major section of the story, Nehemiah 1—7, will again express the conviction that God was responsible for the gracious support of the Persian throne when Nehemiah states, "the king granted me what I

15

asked, for the gracious hand of my God was upon me" (Neh. 2:8).

To a community struggling with questions of the divine disposition, this proclamation offered security and assurance. Without this community response, initiated at God's prompting, the edict of Cyrus would have had little effect. As it was, the response did not include all who were in Babylon. Many had learned to cope and even thrive in the environs of Mesopotamia and so were unwilling to pull up stakes and return to the impoverished conditions of Palestine. That the priestly families comprised a disproportionate ten percent of those who returned is a sobering testimony to the numbers who chose to stay behind. Especially ill-represented were the Levites who may have felt they had little to gain in a secondary role in the Jerusalem temple.

But this should not blind us to the faithful response of those who did set out courageously with Zerubbabel. Their faithful response to the stirring of God can serve as a reminder that there is no redemption without regeneration, and that God can and will work with what is available. Neither should we disparage those who stayed behind, even if for no other reason than that God's primary instruments in the restoration, Ezra and Nehemiah, were both born and nurtured in the faith of families still living in Babylon long after Zerubbabel's initial return.

Concerned as it is to foster an appreciation of the continuity between pre- and postexilic Israel, the text depicts the return from Babylon as a "second exodus." In this depiction the reader is asked to make connections with the prophecy of Second Isaiah, who also spoke of the return in this fashion (Isa. 43:14–21; 48:20–21; 51:10; 52:12).

One of the ways in which the text recalls the exodus is found in the summons to their now-conquered Babylonian neighbors to provide the returnees with silver, gold, and other gifts (vv. 4, 6). This strongly echoes the Exodus theme of "despoiling the Egyptians," which is foreshadowed in Moses' original commission (Exod. 3:21f.), reintroduced in the announcement of the final plague (Exod. 11:2), and fulfilled in the report of Israel's garnering of silver and gold from the Egyptians due to God's gracious provision (Exod. 12:35f.). In both instances their past captors generously met the needs of the people of God, whether for the hazardous journey or for the reestablishment of worship.

A further allusion to the exodus tradition is found in Ezra

16

2:68f., where the provision of material goods by the captors is matched by a "freewill" contribution by some of the leaders of the community toward the rebuilding of the Temple. Exodus 35:21–29 records a similar freewill offering of the people to contribute to the erection of the Tent of Meeting in response to the request of Exodus 25:2–9. The curious mention of the livestock that accompanied the returnees in the verses immediately preceding (Ezra 2:64–67), may be an allusion to the description of the exodus group in Exodus 12:38: "A mixed crowd also went up with them, and livestock in great numbers, both flocks and herds," as well.

In many ways the clearest expression of continuity appears in the material concerning the cultic vessels that Nebuchadnezzar had carried off as war trophies (vv. 7–11; cf. the further elaboration of this theme in Ezra's mission 7:19; 8:25–30, 33–34). The presence of these vessels in the temple of the Babylonian gods had been a graphic reminder of the apparent victory of those gods over Yahweh, the God of Israel. That Babylon understood its possession of the vessels in this way is strongly suggested by Daniel 5:1–4, which relates Belshazzar's toasting the power of his gods with the very vessels that had been removed from Jerusalem. Ironically, it was on this same night that Babylon was captured (Dan. 5:23, 30). The return of those vessels to a fully furnished temple would powerfully symbolize both the restoration of worship and the continuity with the past that the nascent community so desperately needed to see. In addition, any lingering doubts as to God's intention with regard to his people could now be swept away.

Closer examination of this episode reveals that the material framing the actual list that formed the nucleus of the passage is carefully structured to emphasize this movement of the vessels "from Jerusalem . . . . to Jerusalem" (Ezra 1:7–11):

A   Vessels carried away *from Jerusalem* are brought out (7)
  B   Vessels counted out to *Sheshbazzar* (8)
    X   The list of vessels (9–11a)
  B'   Vessels brought up by *Sheshbazzar* (11b)
A'   With exiles from Babylonia *to Jerusalem* (11c)

The structure also emphasizes the precise enumeration of the vessels. Unfortunately such precision does not extend to the textual witnesses we have; the RSV has chosen the 1 Esdras text to ease the numerical difficulties of a Hebrew text (retained in NRSV) that does not add up. The point of this painstaking count-

17

ing out lies in its testimony to the completeness of the restoration as *restoration* and not mere innovation, as the numbering of each utensil proclaims the cultic assurance of God's covenantal continuance with the people.

Important as these allusions to the exodus are for their intended purpose of providing continuity with the past for the restoration community, the differences between the two situations ought not be overlooked. Whereas the exodus concerned the deliverance of Hebrew slaves from the oppression of their cruel masters, those who returned with Zerubbabel left with the considerable support of a king who had conquered their nemesis. Furthermore, the flight from Egypt had resulted in the establishment of a people and an autonomous nation. This political liberation had no such counterpart in the return, which only allowed the reestablishment of the temple and its worship. They were still regarded as "people of the province" (Ezra 2:1), under the jurisdiction of the Persian throne. Instead of a nation that could organize and perhaps vindicate itself, now there could be only a religious entity, a congregation. As such, one of the tasks that Ezra in particular would have to deal with was the reconstitution of the people of God within the political structures of the Persian Empire.

Israel Transplanted (Ezra 2)

Throughout the course of the commentary we shall see that the numerous lists contained in these books serve a very practical purpose. Most simply put, that purpose is to provide the reader with a running commentary on the status of the community in relation to the developing situation of reform. The long register of those who returned with Zerubbabel in Ezra 2:1–70 catalogs those who were, in Kidner's evocative phrase, "the living portions of Israel, roots and all, for transplanting" (p. 36). Though the same list, displaying minor discrepancies, appears with a different purpose in Nehemiah 7:6–73, here it provides a triple emphasis on the restoration community's continuity with the past.

First of all, comparison with its twin listing in Nehemiah 7 suggests that an additional name has dropped out of verse two, that of Nahamani (cf. Neh. 7:7). This would yield a total of twelve names for the leadership of the nation, and while there is no explicit linkage of these men to the twelve tribes, we may take the number as suggestive of a complete restoration of the tribes that formed sacral Israel (vv. 1–2a).

Second, this suggestion is furthered by the observation that the list falls into two carefully delineated sections: (1) a list of those Israelites who could prove their descent from Israel of old whether lay people (vv. 2b–35) or the various cultic officials (vv. 36–58), and (2) a list of those who could not prove their descent, again, further subdivided into laity (vv. 59–60) and clergy (vv. 61–63). Clearly, what is at issue in these lists is the ability of the individuals so listed to trace their continuity with the past, particularly the past that constituted preexilic Israel. This is further emphasized in the curious silence of these lists with regard to individual names in favor of family names, designated not by the present head of the family but by the name of an ancestor in preexilic times (vv. 3–20) or, more generally speaking, by specific preexilic towns (vv. 21–35). The inability of those recorded in verses 59–63 to prove either a familial or geographic tie with the past emphasizes this point in a negative way.

A third indication that continuity with the past was the prime motivation for the inclusion of this list at this point arises from the geographical interest thus displayed. Both the inclusion formed by the mention of "all to their own towns" (vv. 1, 70) and the identification of the returnees with specific towns in verses 21–35 recall the parallel with the original occupation of the promised land as it is related in the latter half of the book of Joshua. There, as here, the land is allocated to the people, according to their towns, under the leadership of a diarchy (Joshua and Eleazar, the priest, Josh. 14:1; Zerubbabel and Jeshua, the priest, Ezra 2:2).

The contemporary reader of the list might wonder why more was not made of the messianic overtones that Zerubbabel's presence would evoke. As the lineal descendant of the royal house and heir to the throne of David (I Chron. 3:19), questions concerning his role in the new community would surely have arisen. This was clearly the case in the prophetic presentations of Haggai and Zechariah 1—8. Was this shoot from the stock of Jesse the promised Messiah so fervently longed for by Isaiah? The text is silent at this point and hints at the growing postexilic notion that Israel was no longer to look to individuals for its salvation. Hezekiah and Josiah had not succeeded in permanently stemming the tide of intransigence, neither would Zerubbabel nor the Maccabees. More and more, postexilic Israel became aware that its hope was to be founded upon the activity of God alone.

Seen in this way, the list loses some of its intractability. It serves the practical purpose of assuring the restoration community that they had not arrived upon the scene from out of the blue but were in fact solidly established upon their ancestral roots as emphasized by their family pedigrees and upon their ancestral home as emphasized by their territorial situation. They were thus not cut off from the ancient promise of land and posterity made to Abraham (Gen. 12:1–3), but rather they were the raw material from which God would now bring forth further fulfillments of that glorious promise.

Ezra 3—6
Continuity and Opposition

After the straightforward account of Ezra 1—2, the narrative takes a tortuous path to its completion in Ezra 6. Failure to take the text's literary composition into consideration has opened a Pandora's box of attempted historical reconstructions as interpreters have sought to understand why material dealing with opposition to the rebuilding of the city and its walls during the later reigns of Ahasuerus (Xerxes) and Artaxerxes (4:6–23) should be included in a discussion of the building of the Temple.

Of crucial importance for the proper interpretation of these chapters is the recognition of two related literary devices, first observed by S. Talmon (pp. 317–328) and followed by Williamson in his commentary, known as "summary notation" and "repetitive resumption." The function of the "summary notation" is to "recapitulate the contents, and thus also delineate the extent of a preceding textual unit" (Talmon, p. 322). Thus, Ezra 4:4–5, which speaks of the people of the land discouraging the people of Judah so that they were afraid to build, does not constitute a new phase in the historical situation, which then has to be variously interpreted, but rather it recapitulates the previous statement of this *literary* development in 3:3 and establishes 3:1—4:5 as a textual unit. As Williamson says:

20

> 4:4–5 will be the narrator's way of explaining that 3:1–6 refers to an altar dedication in the reign of Cyrus, that for fear of the

peoples of the land no building was undertaken at that time,
and that 3:7—4:3 describes the start of the work in the time
of Darius (*Ezra, Nehemiah,* p. 44).

The function of the "repetitive resumption" is to resume a
narrative flow that has been interrupted by the insertion of
digressionary material, by repeating themes or vocabulary
found where the narrative broke off. Thus, by recalling "the
reign of King Darius of Persia" (4:5b), Ezra 4:24 neither marks
a new stage in the historical development of the narrative nor
suggests that Darius followed Ahasuerus or Artaxerxes. Rather,
4:6–23 is marked as a digression providing information on similar, though later, acts of opposition that our literary conventions
would place in brackets or a footnote.

With these literary conventions in mind, it is possible to
outline the general narrative flow of these first six chapters in
the following concentric diagram:

A   Hebrew version of Cyrus Edict to rebuild temple
        (1:1–11)
    B   List of returnees (2:1–70)
      C   Altar worship restored (time of Cyrus) (3:1–6)
      [Temple begun (time of Darius) (3:7—4:3)]
          D   Building stops (4:4–5a; sum. notation of 3:1—4:3)
          [prolepsis to events in Darius's reign (5:1ff.) (4:5b)]
              X   Opposition to building of walls (4:6–23)
          D′   Building stops (rep. resumption of 4:4–5 in 4:24)
      C′   Temple building resumes (5:1–2)
    B′   Demand for list (cf. vv. 3f., 10) (5:3–17)
A′   Aramaic version of Cyrus Edict, temple rebuilt (6:1–22)

The "bulges" contained in C and D, which partially destroy
the overall symmetry of the structure, are occasioned by the
necessity of relating the two distinct activities of altar dedication in the time of Cyrus (3:1–6) and the laying of the temple
foundations in the time of Darius (3:7—4:3), the juxtaposition of
which is used to emphasize the fear of the returnees in explanation of their delay in rebuilding the temple. Haggai offers a
conflicting reason for the delay, namely, the sloth of the people
(Haggai 1:1–8).

Recognition of these literary signposts and the resultant   21
narrative flow of these chapters should also alert the attentive
reader to a recurring problem in the investigation of these
books. Despite our use of this material as our only source for the

history of the restoration, the texts themselves are far more interested in presenting the story of the restoration as it relates to the theological and "pastoral" problems of the community. Proper interpretation must take this theological characterization into account and seek to discern those motivations as the underlying basis of the narrative. Many of the riddles that have bewitched earlier readers, such as the fifty-year gap between Ezra 6 and 7 or the chronological relationship between Ezra and Nehemiah, dissolve once the text is understood to be ordered on theological rather than historical or chronological grounds.

Gunneweg clearly sees the importance of this approach when he notes that the Aramaic section (especially 4:4–24) is not merely an insertion but rather forms the point on which everything turns, in that the opposition there related directs itself against the very sense of the return, which was to come back and restore the temple, thereby reconstituting the exilic community (and not the opposition, who had remained in the land) as the *true* heirs of Israel (*VTS*, p. 154). This passage's placement at the center of our narrative structure confirms Gunneweg's insight.

Thus, the exposition of these chapters will be concerned to explore the twin themes of continuity, as initiated in chapters 1 and 2, and opposition.

First Things First: Worship Restored (3:1—4:5)

The previous chapters were concerned to establish the continuity between pre- and postexilic Israel in terms of God's gracious activity and the physical transplanting of the people themselves. Here the theme of continuity is carried out with reference to worship, that sacred, institutional element of the people's life that would increasingly bind them together in the new community. This continuity is manifested in three ways.

First, it is significant that "the people gathered together" in the "seventh month" (3:1, 6). The seventh month, as the most important of the liturgical year, was especially opportune for embarking on new ventures and appears regularly as a thematic element in this literature (Neh. 7:73b; 8:2; 8:14–18; cf. II Chron. 5:3; 7:8–10). This expression of their unity after the long years of dispersion in Babylon would serve to proclaim their solidarity as a group and cohesion as a people united in the

22

praise of God. The people of God have always appreciated the importance of liturgical worship, in whatever form, for providing the opportunity to express their interdependence under God. But with this restoration of worship on an altar reestablished upon the very site that had lain dormant throughout the long years of exile, the people also reaffirmed their continuity with the sacral traditions of the past. For the first time since the destruction of 587 the offerings prescribed "in the law of Moses the man of God" (Ezra 3:2) were presented to the Lord. Just as the ancient congregation of Israel, upon crossing the Jordan and under this same Mosaic prescription, had placed the newly acquired land of promise under the jurisdiction of God at Mount Ebal, and bound themselves and it to his guidance (Deut. 27:1–8), so now the new congregation confessed their allegiance and dedication upon being returned.

Second, whether by historical coincidence or literary artistry, it is appropriate that the first feast to be celebrated by the community should be the Feast of Booths, which, according to Leviticus 23:42–43, served to commemorate God's gracious deliverance of their forebears from Egypt. The parallels to their own recent history of deliverance would hardly have been missed by the community as they spent the week dwelling under the leaves and boughs that had been specially erected for the occasion in Jerusalem. Contemplation of God's provision in the wilderness, as emphasized by the stark contrast between these makeshift dwellings and their usual homes, would also remind them of the tenuous nature of their current existence in the land and make them doubly aware of their dependence on divine mercy. All of this would be more readily apparent to the newly arrived community who would only just have completed the arduous task of moving into their homes than it is to those of us who enjoy the benefits our far more settled existence affords.

In this regard the dominant character of the feast's celebration, thanksgiving for God's mercy, should not be overlooked. Both the offerings that attended the restoration of worship and the song of thanksgiving that accompanied the laying of the temple foundation solidify the reader's perception that it is the people's awareness of their dependence on God's "steadfast love" that "endures forever toward Israel" (3:11) that is being celebrated.

A third indication of the concern for continuity contained

23

in these paragraphs is the intentional comparison drawn between the present temple and that of Solomon. Then (I Chron. 22:4; II Chron. 2:8), as now (3:7), the cedars of Lebanon were imported for the construction of the edifice, much of the work was apportioned to masons and carpenters from Sidon and Tyre (I Chron. 22:4), and it was paid for in the same way (II Chron. 2:10). Though muted, the prophecy of Isaiah 60:10-14, which speaks not only of the glory of Lebanon but also of the wealth of nations and foreign workers, is definitely alluded to and indicates that the rest of the world is also to render their gifts and talents in the reconstruction as God places them at Israel's disposal. Then (I Kings 6:1), as now (3:8), the work begins "in the second month," and priests and Levites are appointed to oversee the operation (vv. 8b–9; cf. I Chron. 23:4–32).

Despite this deliberate parallel with the First Temple, two items emphasize points of contrast. In the past, pious kings had themselves provided for the restoration of the Temple, just as David and Solomon had themselves borne the financial burden of the cult. But now, for the first time, we see the congregation as a whole coming together in support of the task. That this freewill offering had arisen from feelings of profound gratitude and recognition of God's gracious provision cannot seriously be doubted and serves to illustrate the response that can be expected from evangelical preaching even today.

A second point of contrast has a more bittersweet flavor. The comparisons with Solomon's Temple were intended to encourage the community by establishing points of continuity with the past. Verses 10–11 attest the success of that intention since most of those assembled joyfully praised God at the laying of the foundation. At least some in the group, however, still recalled the splendor of the first temple and were unable to join in the festivities as they were moved to tears by the comparison (vv. 12f.). Since Ezra 6:3 gives only two of the three dimensions recorded for Solomon's Temple in I Kings 6:2 and thus may be corrupt, it is impossible to discern the reason for the weeping that mingled with the joy. Nevertheless, as it stands, the text reminds us, as it did its first readers, that the final, joyous consummation of God's restoration still lies in the future. When these books reach their high point in the dedication of the walls (Neh. 12:27–43), the people will again rejoice, and "the joy of Jerusalem" will again be "heard far away" (Neh. 12:43), but then it will not be mingled with the sound of weeping.

24

Immediately following the description of the community's joyous celebration an ominous chord is sounded in the first five verses of chapter 4, the strains of which will linger throughout much of the narrative. Ironically, this theme of opposition is introduced in what seems to be an offer of cooperation on the part of the leaders of the indigenous population, "Let us build with you [Hebrew: "we will build with you," a much stronger statement]; for we worship your God as you do, and we have been sacrificing to him ever since the days of King Esarhaddon of Assyria who brought us here" (v. 2).

Readers who have carefully followed the text's argument that the restoration was the beginning of God's fulfillment of the great prophetic promises of the exile might be puzzled by Zerubbabel's curt reply, "You shall have no part with us in building a house to our God; but we alone will build to the LORD, the God of Israel, as King Cyrus of Persia has commanded us" (v. 3). Had not those same prophetic voices also spoken of the nations drawing near to walk in the light of the Lord, assist in the building, take part in the sacrifices, and share in the blessing (e.g., Isaiah 60)?

A hint that the text views this offer of assistance with suspicion, however, appears in the opening verse, "When the *adversaries* of Judah and Benjamin heard that the returned exiles were building a temple to the LORD, the God of Israel" (v. 1). Just who these "adversaries" were is not entirely clear, but there is some agreement that they comprised the descendants of those peoples planted in the Northern Kingdom by the Assyrians in accordance with their policy of deportation, following the fall of Samaria in 722 B.C. (v. 10; II Kings 17:1-6). Further information from II Kings 17 suggests that these peoples mixed the worship of their gods with the worship of Yahweh, the God of Israel, and they were even led by an apostate priest from the north, provided by the Assyrians, rather than a true priest from Jerusalem (II Kings 17:24-28). The questionable nature of this basis for the adversaries' claim that they worshiped the God of the returned exiles is also shown by the Deuteronomistic judgment, "So they worshiped the LORD but also served their own gods, after the manner of the nations from among whom they had been carried away" (II Kings 17:33).

Thus, Zerubbabel's reply, which appears far too exclusivistic for our taste, displays a profound insight into the essential nature of the community as well as a judicious understanding

25

of the political necessity for scrupulous adherence to the decree of Cyrus. In Zerubbabel's eyes, for the exiles to have assimilated, even in this apparently harmless way, would have seriously compromised their tentative standing before king and Lord alike, especially after the rigorous sifting of those who were able to prove their ancestry that is represented by the list of chapter two. Yahweh's word was clear: The hard-won insight of the exile, which had transformed disaster into deliverance and horror into hope, was the recognition that God demanded *exclusive* worship, demanded it to the extent that exile was the inevitable outcome of Israel's past disobedience in this regard. For the community to tempt fate at this crucial juncture in this way was theologically impossible. Similarly, Cyrus's word was clear: Official permission to rebuild had been given to them *alone*, and nothing that might jeopardize this political favor could be tolerated. That Zerubbabel's suspicions were justified is made exceedingly clear in the following chapters.

Back to the Future (4:6–24)

This passage has one simple message. The opposition mounted against the construction of the temple in the reign of Darius was analogous to the harassment the rebuilders of Jerusalem would suffer later in the reigns of Xerxes and Artaxerxes. The historical and chronological difficulties that arise when the text's clear literary guideposts are not considered have been discussed above. There it was determined that the function of this parenthetical material is to provide more contemporary examples of the consistent and nearly continuous nature of the opposition that beset the reconstruction. It would be unwise, however, to overlook the importance of this illustrative material, especially since, as Gunneweg maintains and the concentric structuring of Ezra 1—6 shows, it is the point on which the narrative turns.

Reduced to its simplest form, the text consists of a series of letters between the opposition and the Persian throne. The first two of these letters, addressed to Ahasuerus (i.e. Xerxes I, 486–465 B.C.) in verse 6 and Artaxerxes I (465–424 B.C.) in verse 7, are merely mentioned in passing; no response from the king is recorded. Beginning with verse 8, however, a number of changes are introduced. First of all, the language switches from Hebrew to the linguistically similar Aramaic, the official language of the Persian Empire. This shift adds tremendously to the reader's impression that actual sources are being quoted with a consequent enhancement of their impact. Aramaic will continue until 6:18. Of greater significance, both the text of the third letter (the second letter to Artaxerxes I, vv. 8–16) as well as Artaxerxes's reply (vv. 17–22) are presented in full. The close correspondence between the latter two is heightened by the concentric structuring they display:

A Narrative framework listing participants (8–10)
 B Rehum's letter (11–16)
  —address and greeting (11)
  a the Jews are rebuilding the city (12)
   b they will not pay tribute, custom, or toll, impairing the royal revenue (13)
    c a records search will show city's seditious and rebellious nature from of old (14–16)
 B' Artaxerxes' reply (17–22)
  —address and greeting (17)
    c' a records search has shown city's seditious and rebellious nature from of old (18–19)
   b' tribute, custom, and toll were paid to the mighty kings of Jerusalem (20)
  a' decree: the city is not to be rebuilt (21–22)
A' Narrative framework listing participants (23)

Rehum's letter amounts to an accusation by the officials of Samaria, a part of the satrapy of "Beyond the River" (an administrative district that comprised everything west of the Euphrates to the Mediterranean including Judah and Samaria) that the Jews intended to throw off the yoke of Persian authority by rebuilding the walls of Jerusalem. If this accusation were made in or shortly after 448, when the satrap of "Beyond the River," Megabyzus, was actually in revolt, one can better understand the prompt reply from a threatened Persian administration. Throughout the letter Rehum and his cohorts take advantage of this volatile political situation in the empire by fanning the fires of rumor and innuendo.

Three points are made in this regard: (a) The Jews who had recently returned with imperial sanction have congregated at Jerusalem and are currently rebuilding that "rebellious and wicked city" (v. 12). (b) This rebuilding is not as innocent as it sounds. Does the king realize that if the city is refortified the

27

Persian government will no longer be able to collect its expected revenue of "tribute, custom, or toll," to the detriment of the royal treasury (v. 13)? (c) Finally, if the king will but take the trouble to search his own imperial records, he will quickly see for himself the history of rebellion and sedition that has always been a part of this troublesome city, which, in fact, necessitated the destruction of this city in the first place (vv. 14–16).

The trumped-up nature of the accusation is revealed not only by the sly incorporation of such incendiary terms as "rebellious" (vv. 12, 15), "wicked" (v. 12), "hurtful" (v. 15), and "sedition" (v. 15), or by pandering to the fiscal concerns of the crown (v. 13), but also by the exaggerated and impossible claim of the effects such a rebellion by Jerusalem would have: "We make known to the king that, if this city is rebuilt and its walls finished, you will then have no possession in the province Beyond the River" (v. 16).

Nevertheless, the king's prompt, thorough, and positive response (vv. 17–22) attests to the effectiveness of Rehum's letter. His three points are dealt with in reverse order: (c') Yes, a search of the imperial records has substantiated the claim that Jerusalem has a history of rebellion and sedition (v. 19). (b') Indeed, its mighty kings have asserted their independence by collecting tribute, custom, and toll from the entire province of Beyond the River (v. 20). (a') Therefore, we concur in your suggestion that the rebuilding of this city is a serious threat to our holdings in the province and direct you to issue a decree that such activity must cease until further notice (vv. 21–22). The effect of the concentric ordering lies in the emphasis thus placed upon the final decree to prohibit the reconstruction. As we have seen, verse 24 returns us to the place at which the narrative broke off, Ezra 4:5, in preparation for chapters 5 and 6.

A disturbing theological question arises out of this material. After taking such elaborate pains to present the story of the return as the story of God's providential care of his people, why does this section introduce the theme of successful opposition in this vigorous way? Why is the fate of the community, to say nothing of the plan for the restoration, now placed in the heathen hands of Artaxerxes, who, unlike Cyrus who responded to the "stirrings" of God, reacts on the basis of false information received from the enemies of the community? Is God no longer in control? Are the people once again left to their own devices?

The question of God's providential guidance is a major theme in these books. It will reappear in Nehemiah, again in conjunction with opposition. There, as here, it is important to discriminate between different goals in God's plan. On the one hand, a clear proclamation of the divine disposition was needed to encourage a community whose perceptions of God had only recently been turned from despair to hope. The good news of God's intervention on their behalf, in ways analogous to the great redemption of the exodus, reassured their hearts and strengthened their resolve for the arduous task ahead. On the other hand, the nascent community was deeply involved in the process of learning how to be God's people apart from an autonomous political existence, under the sway of foreign power, and in the midst of competing religious perspectives. They had not done well as God's people in the past, even with the external support of political independence. It must be remembered that these books are not content merely to describe the rebuilding of walls and temple. Important as these structures are, without an equivalent growth in the community as well, they become little more than financial burdens.

By means of the struggles and opposition that would continue to beset the community, much-needed spiritual development would blossom and grow. The tentative nature of their existence would highlight their dependence upon God and their need to reconstitute themselves in accordance with the prescriptions laid down in their traditions and creatively applied to their situation. Both of these aspects will occupy much of the later work of Ezra and Nehemiah.

The Temple Reconstructed (Ezra 5—6)

Ominous as the previous chapter had been, chapter 5 returns to the optimistic tone that dominated chapter 3, following the resumption of the narrative in 4:24. The stark contrast with chapter 4 that results from this time shifting serves to emphasize the successful completion of the project while reminding the present community of the dangers and opposition that accompany all endeavors of this sort.

If the reader had wondered about the absence of God and providential care in chapter 4, these chapters unstintingly proclaim God's active presence through the prophetic activity of Haggai and Zechariah (5:1–2; 6:14). Despite the obvious fact

29

that a strictly chronological reading of the unhappy matters related in chapter 4 precludes a historical application of the prophets' words in rebuttal, the proclamation that begins these chapters strikes the reader as extremely bold and daring. The literary arrangement of the text is such that we are meant to take note of this theological statement. Situations of hopelessness can always be effectively refuted by the bold proclamation of God's word.

This must be done judiciously, however. Haggai's castigation of the people's preoccupation with their own affairs in a time of poor crops and inflation (Haggai 1:3–6) and consequent neglect of the temple's rebuilding is passed over in Ezra. No word of judgment or rebuke is recorded. Neither do we read about the political overtones the building of the temple may have had in the turbulent second year of Darius's reign, noted for the upheaval that spread throughout the empire. In the books of Haggai and Zechariah it is clear that hopes for the revival of the monarchy, centered in the person of Zerubbabel, who was of Davidic descent, went hand in glove with hopes for the reconstruction of the temple (Hag. 2:20–23; Zech. 4:6–7). Significantly, this element of the prophetic message is also absent from the Ezra account.

Here, the prophets function as catalysts who enable the rebuilding with their encouraging message (Ezra 6:14) and exemplary conduct: "and with them were the prophets of God, helping them" (Ezra 5:2). This selective utilization of the prophetic message is indicative of the theological and pastoral concern of this passage. The addressees of Ezra 1–6 were in a situation that did not require Haggai's pointed criticism. As the restored community struggling with the difficult question of how one can be faithful to God while living as a subject people, they needed to hear that political autonomy was not a prerequisite for being the people of God. In this context, Haggai's message, as presented in Ezra, could sound an authentic note of God's providential care and encouragement apart from the political revolution that the long digression in chapter 4 had so falsely intimated.

This theological concern is further explored in the material dealing with Tattenai, governor of the province Beyond the River, and his associates (5:3–5; 6:13). While there has been a tendency on the part of older expositors to regard Tattenai's investigation of the Jerusalem proceedings on behalf of the administration as hostile, most recent interpreters regard his efforts as neutral at worst since he did not stop the process of construction during the time it took to receive a ruling on the matter from higher Persian officials.

The text itself offers an explicit theological reason for his leniency: "the eye of their God was upon the elders of the Jews" (v. 5). The use of the imagery of God's "eye" upon the elders may be an intentional furthering of the concept of divine providence (cf. Deut. 11:12; Ps. 33:18f.; 34:15f.). The imagery of God's "hand" that will predominate in these books (Ezra 7:6, 9, 28; 8:18, 22, 31; Neh. 2:8, 18) has more the connotation of a king's royal bounty (cf. I Kings 10:13; Esther 1:7). This presentation of the Persian administration as fair and evenhanded officials is meant to be contrasted with the underhanded deception of Rehum and his cronies in chapter 4. Despite the opposition the people will face, they can count on God and the Persian administration for support.

This overriding theological concern to encourage the community to be the people of God within the political structures that presently obtain becomes even clearer when the literary architecture of this unit is examined carefully. It is striking that these chapters, ostensibly about the building of the temple, consist mostly of correspondence between Tattenai and the Persian throne as regards the proper authorization for the project:

A   Haggai and Zechariah encourage rebuilding of temple
     (5:1-2)
  B   Tattenai et al. inquire about authorization (3-5)
    C   Tattenai's letter of inquiry to Darius (6-17)
    C'   Darius's letter of reply to Tattenai (6:1-12)
  B'   Tattenai et al. comply with authorization (13)
A'   Temple rebuilt as encouraged by Haggai and Zechariah (14-15)

As in chapter 4, narrative material frames the concentric presentation of the correspondence (see below). Both Tattenai's positive portrayal and the selective use of the encouraging aspects of the preaching of Haggai and Zechariah have been discussed above. Before examining the central feature of the correspondence itself, however, a word about the place of the temple in the lives of the people is necessary.

Readers familiar with the prophetic traditions of the Old

31

Testament may be surprised at the positive presentation of the temple that these books display. There is no sense of the dangers inherent in temple worship that exercised so much of the preaching of Amos, Jeremiah, and Third Isaiah. Rather, the temple is seen as a rallying point for the community, a symbol of God's continued presence in their midst, and yet one more indication of the continuity with preexilic Israel that the beleaguered community so desperately needed to see.

Turning to the actual correspondence that forms the heart of these chapters, we see that the two letters have been carefully arranged so that, just as in the correspondence of chapter 4, each point of Tattenai's letter is matched with an explicit response in Darius's reply:

> A   Tattenai's letter of inquiry (5:7–17)
>   a   Report: "Work is being done diligently" (7–8)
>   b   Inquiry as to authorization (9–10)
>   c   Reply of Jewish elders: Cyrus Edict (11–16)
>   d   Request: Search for Cyrus Edict (17)
> A'   Darius's letter of reply (6:1–12)
>   d'   Successful search for Cyrus Edict (1f.)
>   c'   Text of Cyrus Edict (3–5)
>   b'   Darius's authorization (6–12a)
>   a'   Decree: "Let it be done with all diligence" (12b)

Considerable discussion has ensued regarding the historicity of these letters. The duplication of the Cyrus Edict in 6:3–5 has invited comparisons with its earlier appearance in chapter 1, usually with the decision that this version is the more authentic. This in turn has led to a cautious but widespread modern consensus that we are dealing with reliable source materials in these letters. Nevertheless, it must be said that the structural presentation given above raises some suspicion, as does the enthusiastic tone of Darius's reply. Is it possible that Darius would have referred to the sacrifices in such a characteristically Jewish way (6:9–10), to the temple as "this house of God" (vv. 7, 8, 12), or as the place where God "has established his name" (v. 12), *a la* Deuteronomic theology (cf., e.g., Deut. 12:5)? Would he have absolved this subject people in advance, complete with sanctions? Though a Jewish scribe may have been employed to assist in the wording of the reply, it is best to conclude with Blenkinsopp that

32

> the royal reply, with the preceding account of the successful
> archival search, is a free composition elaborated on the histor-
> ical basis of a confirmation of the Cyrus rescript issued during
> the reign of Darius (pp. 126–127).

But then what is the point of this "free composition"? Why
has it been given such a prominent place in the narrative? If the
amount of space given to particular items can be used as a
criterion of their relative importance, attention is immediately
drawn to the Jewish elders' reply to Tattenai's inquiry (5:11–16)
and Darius's authorization of the work (6:6–12a).

The Jewish elders' reply is a model of religious and political
diplomacy. First, they are careful to use terminology that would
be familiar to the Persian officials such as "the God of heaven"
(vv. 11, 12), the use of which in the Old Testament is largely
confined to points of official contact between Jews and Persians,
and "a great king of Israel" (v. 11) in place of "Solomon," with
whom the Persians would hardly have been acquainted. Second, they remain properly deferential in their tone, indicating
that Nebuchadnezzar and the Babylonians had been the instrument of their temple's destruction (vv. 12, 14) while Cyrus had
been the instrument of its reconstruction (v. 13). Their claim is
that they have remained consistently loyal to the Persian re-
gime and are simply carrying out the decree instituted by
Cyrus. Thus, the elders' reply effectively answers the charges of
revolt and sedition made in the correspondence of chapter 4.

Deferential as this reply is, it contains a profound theological understanding of the exile and return. In confessing "because our ancestors had angered the God of heaven, he gave
them into the hand of King Nebuchadnezzar of Babylon, the
Chaldean, who destroyed this house and carried away the
people to Babylonia" (v. 12), the elders demonstrate that the
crucible of the exile has served its intended purpose. The
cause and effect relationship between Israel's national sins and
the tragedy of 587 B.C. had long been recognized in the prophetic tradition, but now it is the people who recognize their
guilt and the justice of God's punishment, thereby taking the
first step on the long journey toward becoming the reconstituted people of God. Their recognition that God had re-
versed this judgment through Cyrus (vv. 14f.) similarly grows
out of an understanding of God's renewed presence among
them, a presence that the rebuilding of the temple will symbolize in an exceedingly concrete manner. This reconstitution

33

of the people, only foreshadowed here, will become Ezra's primary task in the reconstruction.

Darius's reply is nothing less than a full confirmation of Cyrus's permission that immediately precedes it. In fact, it goes beyond the original decree. This is seen in a number of ways. First of all, the version of the Cyrus Edict with which the reply opens (6:3–5) omits the no-longer-relevant permission to return while retaining the necessary decree to rebuild the temple and restore its vessels. Of greater importance is the additional note that the cost is to "be paid from the royal treasury" (v. 4b). This lends an aura of official support to the project. Secondly, Darius adds his own intention to enforce the prescriptions of his predecessor with severe penalties for noncompliance (vv. 11–12a).

Once again, however, there are traces that Darius's reply is also depicted as a rebuff of the adversaries in chapter 4, though again in a literary and not an historical way. McConville notes: "That it is calculated as such (at least by our author) appears from the term "without *delay*" (v. 8), which exactly reverses the state of affairs in 4:24 ("the work . . . *stopped*") by the use of a form of the identical verb" (*Ezra, Nehemiah, and Esther,* p. 39). In addition, the stipulation that the expensive maintenance of the Jerusalem cult was to come from the coffers of the province (vv. 8–10) seems to be directly aimed at the "opposition" of chapter 4.

Thus, by means of his careful presentation, his placement of Jewish terminology in the mouth of the Persian king, and a proleptic rebuff of future opposition, the author subtly makes his point that the will of the God of Israel lies clearly behind the machinations of the empire's political struggles. This affirmation was good news indeed to the ears of his hearers.

Having dealt with the crucial point of Persian authorization, the rest of the narrative unfolds in a natural, uncomplicated fashion. Ending as it had begun with a benevolent administration inspired by the will of God and with guarantees of success from both political and theological spheres, the actual completion of the temple is recounted in a mere three verses (vv. 13–15). By continuing the narrative in Aramaic, the text tacitly acknowledges the community's continuing dependence on the Persians, though in a positive way, in that even they, through their subsidies, participate in the newly established worship of God. The reference to the date, "the sixth year of the reign of King Darius," reminds the reader that now, precisely seventy years after its destruction, the temple is once again ready for worship and celebration.

And celebrate they did! First with a joyful dedication of the temple (vv. 16–18). On the face of it, there was little to account for the joyous nature of the occasion. Given the paltry size of the structure in comparison with Solomon's earlier edifice and especially the magnificent temples of the ancient Near East, in and of itself, the temple would not command attention. Neither would the circumstances that surrounded its completion—the need for permission and assistance from an alien king—be especially uplifting. Nevertheless, the celebration here, as elsewhere in these books, was permeated with joy, as the eye of faith was able to discern the truth that lay behind the physical structure: Their God was with them and for them; continuity with the past was now assured.

As if to emphasize that continuity, the dedication recalls the similar dedication of Solomon's Temple (II Chronicles 7). There, too, the occasion was marked by "joy" (v. 10) and the presence of the priests and Levites at their posts (v. 6). In this context the marked discrepancy in the numbers of sacrificial animals, "hundreds" as compared with Solomon's "thousands," reminds the reader that the community was a mere remnant of the Israel of old. But it was a purified remnant, a chastened remnant that recognized the sin that had forced those who worshiped at Solomon's temple into Babylon as well as the mercy that had now brought them back.

It is significant that in addition to the dedicatory sacrifices they also offered "as a sin offering for all Israel, *twelve* male goats, according to the number of the tribes of Israel" (v. 17). For seventy years, the sin of Israel had gone unatoned. Whether the sacrifice was regarded as a gift to appease an angry God, a substitute bearing the penalty of death, or as a sacred life offering new life to sinners who had forfeited their own, it signaled the cleansing of Israel's national guilt, so long overdue.

The first part of the story of the restoration, Ezra 1—6, concludes with a brief paragraph on the first observance of the Passover and Unleavened Bread by the returned exiles (6:19–22). These feasts were especially appropriate at this juncture of the story, which forms a watershed between the conclusion of the old and the beginning of the new. With the purification of the religious leaders (v. 20) and the community (v. 21), the reinstitution of the offering, and eating of the paschal lamb, a

35

final link is forged in the presentation of the return as a second exodus. The theme of redemption that permeates the Passover resonates with the freedom of God's deliverance from the long years of exile that are now brought to completion.

But there are signs of newness as well, as seen in the significance of the Feast of Unleavened Bread. Just as in the celebration of this feast the people throw out all the old leaven and prepare themselves for the bounty the new grain harvest will provide, so at this turning point in the narrative, as the purified people of God, at worship once again in the land of Israel at their newly completed and dedicated temple, the people throw out the old leaven of their past sinfulness and prepare to walk in the newness that lies ahead.

The theme of exclusivity, which first arose in the careful investigation of lineage in chapter 2 and formed the basis of the community's refusal of the assistance offered in 4:1, is furthered in the application of the term "Israel" to the "returned exiles" (v. 16). These, and these alone, who understand themselves as the purified remnant of Israel of old, can lay claim to being the people of God. As these books progress, this theme of exclusivity will grow increasingly intense, especially in the marriage reforms that will occupy so much of Ezra's and Nehemiah's time. And yet a clear note of tolerance and outreach is sounded in the inclusion of "all who had joined them and separated themselves from the pollutions of the nations of the land to worship the LORD, the God of Israel" (v. 21b), that is, those Israelites who had not experienced exile for whatever reason but who had literally thrown out the old leaven of their lives and now pledged themselves to the faith. Likewise, in Hezekiah's great feasts of Passover and Unleavened Bread following his renewal of the temple, in which members of the North were invited to share in the celebration (II Chron. 30:1ff.), allowance was made for those who were willing to conform to the ideals of purity and worship in Jerusalem.

It was, indeed, a time for joy (vv. 16, 22), and our text closes with three declarations of what God had done to inspire their joyful praise. They provide a fitting summary of the themes of this opening section. The first is that God is the source of their joy: "The LORD had made them joyful" (v. 22). The second is that God is the source of their success and had overcome the opposition to the project by directly influencing the present administration, as he had Cyrus in chapter 1: "The LORD . . . had turned the heart of the king of Assyria to them." Finally, God

36

is the source of their strength so that they could complete the reconstruction of the Temple: ". . . he aided them [literally: "he strengthened their hands"] in the work on the house of God, the God of Israel."

Return Under Ezra and Reconstruction of Community

EZRA 7—10

With the joyous sounds of the Temple dedication and Passover celebration still ringing in our ears, the narrative turns to the second movement in its theological account of the restoration. The brief transition, "After this . . ." (7:1), is deceptive in that it papers over a gap of almost sixty years if Ezra came to Jerusalem in 458 B.C., more if his arrival is to be dated in 428 or 398. The return under Zerubbabel had achieved its goal in the reconstruction of the temple, but Zerubbabel himself had fallen into a black hole of history with no further traces of his subsequent activity. As for the community, the prophetic work of Malachi and Third Isaiah is probably to be dated to this period and provides at least a glimpse of the conditions under which the community lived. This gap in the narrative is yet another reminder that Ezra–Nehemiah is more concerned to present an exposition of the theological significance of the restoration rather than an historical account of the Persian period.

In the perspective of these books, the salient theological moments of the restoration period cohere in three parallel returns—under Zerubbabel (Ezra 1—6), Ezra (Ezra 7—10), and Nehemiah (Neh. 1:1—7:3)—each of which resulted in a different project of reconstruction, namely, the temple, the community, and the walls. All three share a common progression of (1) initial return under the divinely prompted authorization of the Persian crown (Ezra 1:1; 6:22; 7:6, 27f.; Neh. 1:11; 2:4, 8); (2) nearly constant opposition to reconstruction, followed by (3) the overcoming of the opposition with divine aid. Just as the first section had fallen into two major divisions thematically, dealing

37

with the return under Zerubbabel depicted as a second exodus (Ezra 1—2) and the reconstruction of the temple (Ezra 3—6), this second section divides thematically into the return under Ezra, again depicted as a second exodus (Ezra 7—8), and the reconstruction of the community (Ezra 9—10).

Ezra 7—8
The Hand of Their God Was upon Them

At last, after the final editor's long, six-chapter introduction, the text turns to the reformer whose name is enshrined in the title of this book: Ezra, the priest and scribe. While the purpose of these initial chapters is to introduce the reader to the character and concerns of the reformer before his own first-person account begins (7:27), they have been structured to lift up the dominant theological concerns of the postexilic community. As is frequently the case in this literature, a concentric ordering of the material is used to isolate chapters 7 and 8, as a unit dealing with Ezra's return, from chapters 9 and 10, which deal with his reconstruction of the community:

A   Journey to Jerusalem (7:1–10)
  B   Commissioning of Ezra (7:11–26)
    C   Prayer (7:27–28a)
      D   Leaders gathered for journey (7:28b)
        X   Israel Reunited (8:1–14)
      D'   Leaders gathered for journey (8:15–20)
    C'   Prayer and Fasting (8:21–23)
  B'   Commissioning of Vessel Bearers (8:24–30)
A'   Journey to Jerusalem (8:31–36)

As it stands, the narrative is framed by the journey of Ezra and his companions to Jerusalem. This framework and its related narrative threads, which run throughout chapters 7 and 8, heighten the reader's sense of continuity but provide very little information about the journey itself, being content to list the participants and a minimal itinerary. Basically we are told that "this Ezra went up from Babylonia" (Ezra 7:6a), that he was accompanied by "some of the people of Israel, and some of the priests and Levites, the singers and gatekeepers, and the tem-

38

ple servants" (7:7b), that they left Babylonia on the first day of the first month and arrived in Jerusalem in the fifth month of the seventh year of Artaxerxes (7:7–9). On the way, the company camped for three days at the otherwise unknown river Ahava, where the absence of Levitical representatives was first noticed and corrected (8:15–20). The journey was completed without incident due to God's deliverance "from the hand of the enemy and from ambushes along the way" (8:31).

Bare as these bones appear to be, they provide a skeleton for the weightier theological themes that lie at the heart of the text's concerns. These, too, are arranged concentrically within the frame of the journey to Jerusalem. Ezra's commission, which outlines his task and is presented as a letter from Artaxerxes to Ezra in imperial Aramaic similar to the correspondence in Ezra 4—6 (7:11–26), is matched by Ezra's commissioning of the priests and Levites who were to carry the sacred vessels to Jerusalem (8:24–30). His doxological prayer, praising God for moving the heart of Artaxerxes (7:27–28a), finds an echo in the company's fast and prayer for a safe journey (8:21–23). This correspondence of activity, first with Ezra alone, and then with Ezra and the whole company, foreshadows the cooperative, delegatory, administrative style Ezra will later use with great success in his dealings with the community's problems (Ezra 9—10; Nehemiah 8—10). At the heart of the narrative is a list of the families who chose to return with the reformer (8:1–14).

The coherence of the passage is further strengthened by a series of variations on the theme, "the hand of their God was upon them" (7:6, 9, 28; 8:18, 22, 31; cf. Neh. 2:8, 18). The first three references, couched in the singular, occur at strategic moments in Ezra's personal preparation, while the last three, couched in the plural, refer to the preparation of the company as a whole, effectively highlighting God's gracious benediction over both the personal and corporate aspects of the journey.

NARRATIVE CONCERNS

Since the primary function of these chapters is to lay the theological groundwork for the subsequent presentation of Ezra's work in Ezra 9—10 and Nehemiah 8—10, the following comments will examine the overlap among three narrative concerns that will prove to be programmatic for the theological depiction of his work: (1) Ezra as priest and scribe, (2) the question of the law, and (3) the portrayal of the return as a second exodus. This will be followed by a brief discussion of the theological implications of these chapters.

Ezra the Priest and Scribe. Clearly, the overriding narrative concern of these chapters is to provide the reader with an introduction to the person and mission of Ezra. It is important to note that, once again, the flames of revival were kindled and fanned not in the environs of Jerusalem but in the exilic setting of Babylon. The previous return under Zerubbabel with explicit authorization from Cyrus had originated in the same place, as would the third return, under Nehemiah. These books consistently claim that those members of the community who had personally experienced the trauma of exile were the seedbed from which the restored community would grow.

We have seen the careful downplaying of Zerubbabel's messianic credentials in contrast to their explicit heralding in the preaching of Haggai and Zechariah. That stance will continue here, and readers will have to await the coming of the true Messiah in Jesus the Christ for a continuation of Israel's messianic expectations. In these chapters, Ezra's impressive qualifications regarding an alternative foundation for the community—the Torah and the priesthood—receive the emphasis.

With regard to the priesthood, readers cannot fail to notice that the initial report of the journey to Jerusalem (7:1–10) barely begins before it digresses into a stylized genealogy of Ezra, the purpose of which is to make clear that Ezra, though not himself the high priest, was a member of the priestly line that had provided Israel's high priests in the past (7:1b–5). That this identification is uppermost in the mind of the compiler is revealed in four ways:

1. If the omission of six names that occur in the corresponding genealogy in I Chronicles 6 (the names between Azariah and Meraioth in Ezra 7:3) is intentional and not merely the result of scribal error, the list is shortened to include only those names that are necessary for continuity (see below).

2. The fact that Seraiah (v. 1) could not have been Ezra's "father," in that at least 120 years separated these two, points to Seraiah's office as the last high priest in Jerusalem before the Babylonian captivity (I Chron. 6:14) as the reason for the list's beginning at this point. The compiler omitted the three or four intervening generations to Ezra because the exile precluded their serving as high priests.

3. The termination of the list at "the chief priest Aaron" (v.

5), rather than Levi as in I Chronicles 6, again shows that it is the high priestly office that is being emphasized, not the line of descent.

4. The Masoretic accentuation isolates Ezra and Aaron from the remaining names, yielding the following arrangement:

Ezra, reconstitution of Mosaic system
   seven priests to destruction of temple
      Azariah, first priest in Solomon's temple
   seven priests before construction of temple
Aaron, first chief priest

When it is observed that there are seven names of priests who served before the construction of the temple, between "the chief priest, Aaron" (v. 5b), founder of the Levitical system, and Azariah, "who served as priest in the house that Solomon built in Jerusalem" (I Chron. 6:10), as well as seven names of priests who served until the temple's destruction between Azariah and Ezra, the priest and scribe responsible for the reconstitution of the Mosaic system, it becomes clear that the genealogy has been carefully arranged to establish Ezra's credentials, especially as they relate to the compiler's situation. The growing importance of the high priestly office in the compiler's contemporary political climate, as well as the traditional priestly functions of guardian and teacher of the Law, made the establishment of these credentials imperative. In addition, the genealogy continues the theme of displaying the community's continuity with the past that was so important in Ezra 1—6.

Important as the establishment of Ezra's priestly credentials was, however, the rest of the narrative is strangely silent about this aspect of the reformer. Only the necessity of priestly involvement in the sanctification of the temple vessels and the commissioning of their bearers (8:24–30) recalls Ezra's status. In terms of the later narrative, Ezra is depicted as a scribe, that is, a student and teacher of the law. Unfortunately, just what this office entailed is shrouded in mystery. In all probability, his title "scribe of the law of the God of heaven" (Ezra 7:12, 21), was an official Persian designation in which "scribe" meant something like our term "secretary" and "law of the God of heaven" was official Aramaic nomenclature for the Jewish religion. Thus, Ezra functioned in the Persian court as a "secretary of Jewish affairs," and his mission to Jerusalem was as an official representative of the king.

The text, capitalizing on the presence of the term "scribe,"

41

has apparently transferred its rather different contemporary understanding of that term, as it had developed in the second temple period, back onto Ezra, thereby enshrining him as the first and greatest exemplar of that office. Ezra is portrayed as the perfect second temple scribe who "had set his heart to study the law of the LORD, and to do it, and to teach the statutes and ordinances in Israel" (7:10). With these words the transformation is complete.

By choosing to retell the story of Ezra in this way, the compiler has theologized an originally secular mission on behalf of the Persian crown, with the result that readers of this text are invited to see in Ezra's return the second movement in God's plan for the return and restoration of God's people.

The Law. A second narrative concern is closely related to the first. After introducing the reader to the person of Ezra, the narrative presents his mission in the form of a letter from Arta-xerxes commissioning him to go to Jerusalem (7:11–26). After the usual introduction and greetings, including permission for all who so desire to return with Ezra (vv. 12f.), the letter falls into the following thematic structure:

A   Mission: inquiry concerning "the law of your God, which is in your hand" (v. 14)
  B   Gifts for the temple from Babylon (vv. 15–18)
    X   Vessels and funding for the temple service to be provided from the royal treasury (vv. 19–20)
  B'   Gifts for the temple from the province (vv. 21–24)
A'   Mission: teach knowledge of "the wisdom of your God which is in your hand" (v. 25f., RSV)

Ezra is given responsibility in two discrete areas: for the Temple, comprising the gathering and transportation of gifts, funding, and reception of vessels from the king and the residents of Babylon, as well as from the residents of the province Beyond the River (vv. 15–24), framed by responsibility for the law, which included making an inquiry as to its status among the Jerusalem community (v. 14) and seeing to its implementation through the establishment of judicial magistrates and teachers (vv. 25–26).

Immediately following the text of the letter, Ezra gives thanks to God but only for moving the heart of Artaxerxes to beautify the temple (7:27–28a). The latter half of chapter 8 records his carrying out of that charge. The first problem to be dealt with concerned the lack of Levitical representation

42

among those who returned (8:15–20). Ezra sent a delegation to Casiphia (also otherwise unknown) to recruit Levites for the journey. It would be a mistake to emphasize the paltry number of those who responded. Rather, like Ezra or the compiler, one should view the response as a testimony to the gracious activity of God on behalf of the mission since it was by "the gracious hand of our God upon us" that thirty-eight Levites decided to join the caravan (v. 18).

The ensuing narrative, however, will relate his tireless activity on behalf of the law (Ezra 9—10; Nehemiah 8—10). There is a tension here. The usual interpretation of Ezra's activity regarding the law identifies that law with some version of the Torah (either the entire Pentateuch, the D legislation, the P legislation, or some combination of the two), which Ezra supposedly brought back to Jerusalem and implemented as the new basis for the community. The assumed necessity of the immediate fulfillment of this commission becomes the primary evidence for the widely accepted reconstruction of moving Nehemiah 8 after Ezra 8. There are several factors that militate against this understanding.

1. The Aramaic word *dat,* translated as "law" in these chapters (7:12, 14, 21, 25, 26), usually relates to royal decrees, as seen in the books of Esther and Daniel, and so should not be taken to be an Aramaic equivalent for Torah.

2. We have seen that the compiler has infused the secular term "scribe" with the developed, theological meaning of that term in his contemporary, Second Temple situation, so that the designation of Ezra as "scribe of the law of Moses" (7:6) is not to be understood as a translation of Ezra's title but rather as a theological foreshadowing of his scribal activity in Nehemiah 8:1.

3. We have also seen that "the law of the God of heaven" (7:12) is official Persian nomenclature for the Jewish religion and so cannot be equated with the Torah.

4. That this law that Ezra brings to Jerusalem cannot be a "new" law, as represented by some recent recension of the Pentateuch by Ezra or other exilic priests, is clearly shown by the text itself, which twice assumes that it is already known to the inhabitants of Jerusalem (Ezra 7:25, where Ezra is commanded to judge "all . . . who know the laws of your God," and Neh. 8:1, where *the assembly* asks Ezra to read from the "book of the law of Moses," with no prior mention of that book).

Thus, the text is silent about the identification of the law

43

that Ezra brought with him to Jerusalem. Historically his mission was secular in nature as was his office as a scribe or secretary in the Persian court. The description of the law as being "in [his] hand" (7:14, 25) is not to be taken literally, as though he actually carried a scroll from Babylon, but figuratively with the meaning "which you possess" (cf. NRSV). Nevertheless, it is also clear that the compiler has capitalized on the differing ways the terms "scribe," "law," and "in your hand" would be heard by his community and invites the reader to hear this text as if it were a report of Ezra, the scribe (in the later Jewish sense) mandated to implement the Torah of his God. This theological claim of the text, regardless of its historical accuracy, is at the heart of the passage as we now have it and will control the reading of Ezra's subsequent reforms in both Ezra 9—10 and Nehemiah 8—10.

A Second Exodus. A third narrative concern has to do with the compiler's studied attempt to present all three returns as a second exodus in fulfillment of the exilic prophecy of Second Isaiah (42:13–16; 43:14–21; 52:1f., 11f.) through the use of careful allusions to the first exodus. Among these allusions are the following:

1. Klaus Koch draws attention to the cultic nature of the return. He points out the repetition of the technical terms for the exodus that occur in these chapters (*'alah*, "to go up," Ezra 7:6, 7, 8:1; and *ma'alah*, "going up," 7:9, RSV margin), and he provides a plausible explanation of the force of *ki*, "because," in 7:10, a word that is problematic in other interpretations. According to Koch, verses 8 and 9 (dealing with the date of Ezra's departure) are closely connected with verse 10 (the idealized portrait of Ezra as a second temple scribe) by the causal use of *ki*. In other words, Ezra chose to leave when he did *because* his study of the Torah had uncovered the first day of the first month as the time of the Passover festival commemorating the first exodus (Exod. 12:2). Thus, Ezra's departure on that same day would coincide with the original event. Koch assumes this was Ezra's own contribution. In the light of the compiler's other theological recasting of the story, however, it seems more likely that this (and the other allusions) derive from him and not Ezra. We have already had occasion to remark upon a third indication of the cultic nature of the return, namely, that the delay by the river Ahava in order to involve a token number of Levites is intelligible "only against the back-

ground of the order of the march through the desert after the original Exodus. In accordance with the P source (Num x.13ff.), there must be Levites with special tasks, as well as priests and laymen, with Ezra also" (Koch, p. 187).

2. The theme of "despoiling the Egyptians" has also been used extensively in Ezra–Nehemiah to support the compiler's typological linking of the returns and the first exodus. Here, the material dealing with the financial support of the temple (7:14–20, especially vv. 15f.) can be seen as an extension of this pervasive theme.

3. With regard to the journey itself, two allusions contribute to the overall presentation of Ezra's return as a second exodus. At the beginning of the journey, the company's prayer for "a straight way" (8:21, RSV; NRSV: "a safe journey" misses the allusion) recalls Second Isaiah's memorable prophecy, "In the wilderness prepare the way of the LORD; make straight in the desert a highway for our God" (Isa. 40:3). At the end of the journey, the company's three-day rest (8:32) reproduces the three-day rest of the Israelites prior to their crossing of the Jordan (Josh. 3:2).

4. An important aspect of Ezra's commission entailed the appointment of judges and magistrates to oversee the judicial responsibilities of the community (7:25f.). This aspect of Ezra's commission is left unmentioned in the remainder of the narrative. It does allude, however, to Moses' delegation of authority in this regard (Exod. 18:13–27) and so contributes to the view that the compiler intends the return to be seen as a second exodus.

5. There is an unusual concentration upon the number twelve in chapter 8, as well. The register of those returning with Ezra (8:2–14) lists twelve families of Israelites after mentioning the priestly families of Phineas and Ithamar, and the royal family of David. Similarly, Ezra commissions twelve priests and twelve Levites (Sherebiah, Hashabiah, and ten of their kinsmen) to transport the vessels to the temple (8:24). At the sacrifice of thanksgiving marking the conclusion of the chapter, the number twelve is also conspicuous. Twelve bulls are offered for all Israel; ninety-six (8 × 12) rams, seventy-two (6 × 12) lambs (reading I Esdras 8:26; MT, NRSV, and RSV read "seventy-seven"), and twelve goats are offered as a sin offering (8:35).

6. This concern for worship is a final allusion to the exodus

typology. Just as the motivating reason for the exodus was to allow the proper worship of God and not the mere freeing of the people from bondage, so here, in the second exodus, it will not be enough simply to restore the people of God to their homeland.

THEOLOGICAL IMPLICATIONS

The intention of Ezra 7—8 is to provide the reader with an introduction to the person and mission of Ezra. This is accomplished by means of a travel narrative relating the journey from Babylon to Jerusalem, including an account of Ezra's commission and a list of those who accompanied him. We have just seen, however, that closer investigation of how the material has been presented reveals its deeper significance.

The text can be read on two levels. On a purely historical reading, Ezra is presented as an official member of the Persian court, with the title "secretary of Jewish affairs," who was sent to Jerusalem at the self-centered request of the king, to implement the Jewish law among those Persian subjects who were of the Jewish faith. Nevertheless, for readers living 160 years after Ezra's mission, the key terms "priest," "scribe," and "law" would be heard with the contemporary meaning those terms had acquired in the early second Temple period. The compiler's theologically motivated restructuring of Ezra's genealogy to emphasize the reconstitution of the Mosaic system, the ambiguity of Ezra's office and what "law" was to be implemented, as well as his typological casting of the return as a second exodus would encourage those readers to see in this account much more than the mere reporting of a Persian fact-finding mission. From those insights, two that center on the grace of God and human response may be lifted up.

Like the list in Ezra 2, the list of returnees found at the heart of the narrative (8:1–14) would be heard by the community as a proclamation of the grace of their God, who had preserved his people during the rigors of the exile as a remnant that would return. The reappearance of the same twelve family names (reading with the NRSV margin) that had returned with Zerubbabel eighty years before, read in conjunction with the compiler's emphasis on the number twelve elsewhere in these chapters, suggests that these twelve families represent the twelve tribes of Israel now finally reunited in the promised land.

46

Its special significance, however, is to be found in the subtle differences this register displays. Ezra 2 had used the names of the families to which those returning exiles belonged as a means of identification. Here, the list is enhanced by the addition of the names of the heads of those families. With regard to the situation of the community, this may imply that there was a growing awareness that membership in the congregation was not entirely a function of nationality as represented by belonging to a particular tribe or family. Rather, the individual adherence to the faith by those members of the family responsible for the decision-making process is given equal importance.

The addition of the names of the family heads also implies continuity. It has been maintained throughout this commentary that the long lists of names, so characteristic of Ezra–Nehemiah, serve the very practical purpose of providing a running commentary on the status of the community in relation to the developing situation of reform. The list in Ezra 2 was important for maintaining the continuity of the restoration community with the past. The addition of the names of the family heads expands that expression of continuity into the present. The gap between the preexilic community and the present congregation had now been bridged and the stage was set for Ezra's reform and reconstruction of the congregation along the lines of the Torah.

This suggests a further theological implication of these chapters, namely the claim that reform (as seen in Nehemiah 8—10) as well as reconstruction of the people (as seen in Ezra 9—10) are impossible apart from the word of God. The nascent community in Jerusalem that had returned with Zerubbabel appeared to have all the earmarks of success. Their return from exile in response to the stirring of their God (Ezra 1:5) carried the blessing of the Persian king in response to a similar divine stirring (1:1). Their reestablishment in the promised land and reconstruction of the temple as the site of their reinstituted worship had succeeded against considerable opposition, again due to God's assistance (6:22). Nevertheless, neither their privileged position in Jerusalem nor the divine blessing that accompanied them immunized them from the neglect of the law that necessitated Ezra's ministry. Conversely, Ezra's secular position in Babylon, far removed from the temple and its worship, did not preclude his calling to be God's agent of reform and reconstruction. This can only be attributed to his determination

47

to "study the law of the LORD, and to do it, and to teach the statutes and ordinances in Israel" (7:10), in conjunction with the empowerment of "the hand of the LORD his God" which "was upon him" (7:6, 9, 28a).

The text thus challenges the community, as it challenges us, to make a similar commitment to study, to do, and to teach but always in humble dependence on the blessing of God for success.

Ezra 9—10
The Judgment of Grace

Sometimes our sensitivity with regard to certain issues impedes our hearing the intended message of biblical passages. These concluding chapters of Ezra are a case in point. We recoil at what seem to be overly harsh measures taken against those members of the community who had intermarried with the indigenous population. We indignantly question the lack of provision made for the unfortunate women who were so summarily dismissed, to say nothing of their children, for whom this must have been an incomprehensible action. If Ezra was "appalled" (9:3) at the marriages, we are equally appalled at the racial overtones carried in his solution.

Our ability to hear this text is further hampered by the complicated history of its composition. With good reason, the overwhelming majority of scholars place Ezra's reading of the law (Neh. 7:73b—8:18) between Ezra 8 and Ezra 9. The present shape of the text thus obscures the original intention of the narrative, as penned by Ezra in his memoir, to present the leaders' confession as a response to Ezra's efforts to make the newly re-introduced law the basis of the restored community, and it prompts the question, "To what cause do we attribute the leaders' change of heart?"

Cogent as these observations about the text may be, they provide very little help in understanding the passage as we now have it. Our first task will be to try to make some sense of the narrative as it stands and then to evaluate its troubling "solution" in the light of Ezra–Nehemiah and Scripture as a whole.

NARRATIVE STRUCTURE

Concentric structuring of the narrative is especially pronounced in these chapters. The overall plan consists of six well-defined elements arranged around Shecaniah's confession and request for action in 10:1–4:

A   Report of the problem of intermarriage (9:1–2)
  B   Ezra's public mourning (9:3–4)
    C   Ezra's prayer (9:5–15)
      X   Shecaniah's confession and request for action (10:1–4)
    C'   Ezra's exhortation and the people's oath (10:5)
  B'   Ezra's private mourning (10:6)
A'   Resolution of the problem of intermarriage (10:7–17) and list of those who had married foreign women (10:18–44)

As it stands, the narrative begins with the community's report of the problem of intermarriage and concludes with the resolution of that problem and a catalog of the offenders. Within this framework, Ezra's public and private mourning testify to the seriousness of the problem in his eyes and provide us with a glimpse into the pastoral concern of the reformer as he displays the extent to which he has made the community's situation his own. Ezra's long prayer serves as a theological reflection on the condition of the newly restored community. Like the other prayers of Ezra–Nehemiah, it is difficult to decide where to draw the line between prayer addressed to God and sermon addressed to the people (and implicitly to the reader!). That the community understood itself as being so addressed is indicated by their oath "to do as had been said" (10:5), as well as Shecaniah's confession and request for action at the heart of the narrative. Throughout these chapters, the key word "faithlessness" *(ma'al)* occurs five times (9:2, 4, 10:2, 6, 10), enhancing the coherence of the passage and drawing the reader's attention to this seminal problem in the community.

The text is further structured by Ezra's movements. Following the initial report, Ezra "sat appalled" (9:3) and then "rose" only to "fall on his knees" in prayer (9:5). "While Ezra prayed" (10:1), the community gathered, and Shecaniah made his confession and request for action. In 10:5 Ezra "arose" again and exhorted the people to make their oath of compliance,

49

whereupon he "withdrew" (10:6) into private mourning as the rest of the people were gathered. Finally, he reappeared and "stood up" (10:10) to address the assembled community.

This structuring of the narrative suggests two things. First, since the individual "scenes" are introduced by the various posturings of Ezra, the reader is invited to rely upon him as an interpretive barometer of the community's response. Second, Ezra's activity is confined to expressions of mourning (9:3f.; 10:6), prayer (9:6–15), exhortation (10:5; 10f.), and selection of the committee responsible for adjudicating the problem (10:16). This highlights the activity of the community that is responsible for bringing the problem to Ezra's attention (9:1f.), demanding a rededication of the community to covenantal faithfulness (10:1–4), and suggesting that the community leaders be responsible for the administration of the solution (10:12–14). Thus, the decision arises out of the community. It is not a decision imposed upon the community by Ezra. As such, the reader senses that there is hope for the restoration community, that change and repentance are possible, and that this new attitude is indicative of the changed heart of the community itself in response to the gracious word of God.

NARRATIVE CONCERNS

The overriding narrative concern of these chapters, and the one that may explain the final editor's displacement of Nehemiah 7:73b—8:18 from its original position immediately before Ezra 9, is to depict this episode as one of a series of reforms undertaken by Ezra and Nehemiah leading to the climactic reading of the law and subsequent renewal of the covenant in Nehemiah 8—10. In the overall presentation of the story of the restoration, the renewal of the covenant receives added emphasis from this juggling of the chronological order of events. That this provides another example of the final editor's tendency to provide a *theological* rather than an *historical* retelling of the story is clear. In addition, we are to read this passage with this contextual priority in mind and seek to uncover the underlying theological message of the text as it relates to that renewal.

In the overall structure of Ezra–Nehemiah these chapters depict the first phase of Ezra's activity as regards the congregation. Here, he works at the negative strengthening of their life under the law. The dismissal of foreign wives, in conformity with the law, will result in a religious purification. This negative strengthening of the congregation's life under the law will be matched by a positive strengthening in the second phase of Ezra's activity, the covenant renewal described in Nehemiah 8—10.

A second narrative concern of these chapters is the studied attempt to continue the presentation of Ezra's return, already begun in chapters 7—8, as a "second exodus." Ezra–Nehemiah's careful presentation of the parallel returns of Zerubbabel (Ezra 1—6) and Nehemiah (Neh. 1—7:3) in this way as well strongly justifies the reader's sensitivities to this patterning and serves as a springboard for further reflection. Among these allusions to the first exodus are the following.

1. A recurrent reason for the people's failure to comply with the stipulations of the covenant at the time of the first exodus was the attraction the ways of Canaan held for them and the degree to which they willingly adopted those practices and incorporated them into their own religious life. The report of the problem of intermarriage, which describes the people's failure to "separate themselves from the peoples of the land" (9:1f.), echoes the same tendency on the part of Israel in Ezra's day. That this parallel is in fact intended may be seen in the character of the list of peoples indicted by the officials. The Hittites, Perizzites, Jebusites, and Ammonites were no longer in existence at this time. By taking action specifically against marriages with Israel's old enemies of the wilderness and conquest periods, the narrative seeks to reestablish in Ezra's day the "conquest" of the Promised Land. The otherwise inexplicable addition of "the Egyptians" to this list strengthens the reader's perception that the list is a "flashback" to the similar situation that existed at the time of the first exodus (cf. Exod. 3:8; 13:5; Deut. 7:1; 20:17).

2. The references to "slavery" and being "slaves" (9:8, 9) strongly recall the lament of the people in Egypt that prompted God's gracious response of deliverance in the exodus.

3. The collage of quotations artfully pasted together in verses 10–12, though most closely associated with Deuteronomy 7:1–3, alludes to the entering of the Promised Land in verse 11.

4. Finally, Ezra's identification with the people throughout his confession of their national sin (*"our* guilt," *"our* iniquities," *"we* have forsaken thy commandments," *"our* evil deeds") re-

51

calls Moses' identification with the people and their sin in Exodus 34:9.

A third narrative concern of these chapters is the writer's attempt to convince the reader that the primary cause of God's rejection of Israel in the past, "faithlessness" *(ma'al)*, is now the primary obstacle to the full restoration of Israel in the present. This accusation of "faithlessness" is strongly theological. The other occurrences of this term in the Old Testament all appear in late texts that reflect upon Israel's exilic situation and describe the sins of believers, that is, members of the covenant community, never unbelievers. In fact, two of these references (Ezek. 39:23 and Dan. 9:7) explicitly attribute the cause of Judah's exile to "faithlessness" ("treachery," NRSV). As J. G. McConville notes in a different context, this word is "normally reserved for serious sin against God, often associated with idolatry, and carrying with it extreme penalties (e.g., Ezek. 14:13; 15:7f.). It is the *seriousness,* rather than particular *kinds,* of sin that the word connotes" (*I & II Chronicles,* p. 17, emphasis added). As we have seen, the fivefold repetition of this term in these chapters (Ezra 9:2, 4; 10:2, 6, 10) is the underlying structural device that unifies the passage. In the context of the story, this "faithlessness" specifically has to do with intermarriage, and it becomes the thematic engine that drives the narrative.

Ezra's Prayer: The Judgment of Grace (9:1—10:1a)

Ezra's magnificent prayer is rightly regarded as the theological high point of the book that bears his name. Here, the themes that have propelled the narrative up to this point receive their definitive interpretation. The prayer, with its framing narrative action, falls into the following structure:

A   Narrative action: Ezra's mourning (9:3–5)
  B   General confession (9:6–7)
    C   Present evidence of divine mercy (9:8–9)
      X   Specific confession (9:10–12)
    C'   Questioned continuance of divine mercy (9:13–14)
  B'   General confession (9:15)
A'   Narrative action: Ezra's mourning (10:1a)

The argument of the prayer proceeds in an orderly fashion. It begins with a general confession of Israel's sinfulness throughout history. "From the days of our ancestors to this day we have been deep in guilt" (v. 7a). That sinfulness ultimately led to the exilic nightmare of being "handed over to the kings of the lands, to the sword, to captivity, to plundering, and to utter shame" (v. 7b.).

These manifestations of the exilic situation are thoroughly consonant with those depicted in that other great account of Israel's fall, the Deuteronomistic History. In contrast to that work's open-ended "wait-and-see" conclusion, however, Ezra's prayer goes on to remind the community that God had not abandoned them. Despite the obviously deserved nature of their punishment, the restoration community had experienced an unexpected measure of divine grace, a "reviving" reminiscent of Ezekiel's graphic vision of the revival of dry bones, mercifully extended to them that they might "set up the house of our God, to repair its ruins and give us a wall in Judea and Jerusalem" (vv. 8–9).

It is important to recognize that Ezra's qualification of God's grace as *"for a brief moment"* (v. 8) emphasizes the tenuous nature of the community's position rather than God's merciful activity. This is all the more striking when it is remembered that scripture usually reserves such qualifications for God's wrath, which lasts for a brief moment, while grace and steadfast love last forever (cf. Isa. 54:7–8). Here, just the reverse is being claimed. The precarious state of the community is further emphasized by Ezra's choice of metaphors in his description of their situation. RSV's "a secure hold" (v. 8) wrongly gives an impression of permanence that the Hebrew "tent-pin" (cf. NRSV, "a stake") does not necessarily convey. The same holds true for the *"little* reviving" of verse 8 (cf. NRSV "sustenance"), and the *"some* reviving" of verse 9 (cf. NRSV "new life," which misses the force of the "some"). The special Hebrew word chosen for "protection" (*gader,* "wall," cf. RSV margin and NRSV; though "fence" or "hedge" better captures the idea of impermanence) is elsewhere found in agricultural contexts (cf. Isa. 5:5) and is not to be confused with Nehemiah's later fortifications of the city. He thus speaks not to bolster the faith of the community but to portray the hazardous nature of their condition.

The question that dominates the prayer, whether this unanticipated reviving could be expected to continue, is first raised in the specific confession of the sin of intermarriage, which,

53

along with the pastiche of prophetic witnesses to God's command against such practices, throws the sin of the present community into strong relief over against the gracious provision of God and forms the turning point of the prayer (vv. 10–12).

At this point, the tone becomes decidedly homiletical as Ezra recaps the argument so far ("seeing that you, our God, have punished us less than our iniquities deserved and have given us such a remnant as this," v. 13) and confronts the community with two rhetorical questions designed to drive home the dire consequences of the community's continued mocking of God's commands (v. 14).

The prayer ends, as it began, with a general confession of Israel's guilt, a confession rendered even more pathetic by the accompanying affirmation of God's righteousness (v. 15).

The most striking feature of the prayer is that it contains no explicit petition, no request for God to continue his gracious providing, not even an appeal for forgiveness. It is pure confession laced with strong homiletic overtones. Thus, the prayer seeks to impress upon the community the seriousness of the situation by reminding them of their sinful solidarity with preexilic Israel and the grave consequences of their guilt. It speaks against an attitude of cheap grace that has counted on God's continual provision but has failed to heed the warnings of scripture or history. The doxology of judgment contained in verse 15, "O LORD, God of Israel, you are just, but we have escaped as a remnant," forms an explicit warning to the community, though in an elliptical fashion. The usual meaning of "just" *(saddiq)* carries connotations of *"graciously righteous,"* so that the doxology should not be paraphrased to say *only,* "As a strict judge, O LORD, you must act against this sinful community, for we remain a remnant that has *merely* escaped." While this thought is clearly present and testifies to the depth of Ezra's faith, a faith that could praise God's justice despite the dire consequences of that justice for the community, Ezra also seeks to argue that no one can question the *mercy* of this God who in righteousness has not caused Israel to be utterly ruined. The more blameless God is shown to be, the more deserving of punishment Israel becomes, as Isaiah so poignantly realized at the time of his call (Isa. 6:1–5). In short, "the prayer doth also preach" and confronts the people with the *judgment of grace.*

54

The Community's Response (10:1b–44)

Ezra's confession, just completed, was a complex mixture of prayer and proclamation. As prayer, its goal was to lament the consistent nature of Israel's sinful response culminating in a doxology of judgment that simultaneously praised God's justice and marveled at the seemingly endless nature of God's mercy. As proclamation, its goal was to convict the community of its sin and motivate it to repent. Again, the reader is allowed a glimpse into the pastoral way Ezra deals with the community. He knows that enforcing the law, under the auspices of his commission from the Persian king, at best could only result in outward compliance. True reformation would only result from confession arising out of the community itself as it became aware of its guilt. That Ezra was successful in his task is clearly presented in the sequel to the prayer (Ezra 10:1b–17), where the community, depicted as responding in just this way with only four dissenting voices (v. 15), becomes the primary focus. The concentric structuring of the narrative, which depicts the community or its representatives as providing leadership in all but verses 6 and 10f., serves to emphasize their self-determining role:

A   Covenant to "send away" foreign wives (1b–4)
  B   People take oath to "do as had been said" (5)
    C   Ezra mourns faithlessness *(ma'al)* (6)
      D   All Israel summoned to Jerusalem in three days (7–8)
      D′   All Israel gathered to Jerusalem in three days (9)
    C′   Ezra convicts of faithlessness *(ma'al)* and urges confession (10–11)
  B′   People do as had been said (12–17)
A′   Foreign wives are "sent away" (18–44)

While the community has clearly taken upon itself the responsibility for rectifying the situation, Ezra is still in control. He makes the people promise to abide by the as-yet-unstated conditions of the solution (v. 5), reminds them of the "faithless" nature of their guilt (v. 10), urges their corporate confession of sin (v. 11), and selects certain leaders of the community to oversee the proposed procedure. But his control is that of an able administrator who facilitates the smooth running of an organization through delegation of authority. Because of this, the community is allowed to experience the benefits that deci-

55

sions one makes for oneself, as opposed to decisions handed down by others, can provide.

THEOLOGICAL IMPLICATIONS

As canonical scripture these chapters engage readers in two major ways: the question of divorce and the need for continual reformation.

With regard to the question of divorce, contemporary readers of this material are frequently scandalized by the harsh measures taken by the restoration community. It must be admitted at the outset that these measures are extreme by the standards of both Testaments. But the text says nothing about the matter that gives rise to the greatest outrage today, the lack of provision for the divorced women and their children. Probably these unfortunates would have returned to their own families who would then have taken responsibility for them. We simply do not know what provisions were made, if any, since the text is concerned with other matters.

In the Old Testament, divorce was permitted (Deut. 24:1), though it was considered a serious undertaking and one which God "hated" (Mal. 2:16). The central issue here, however, is theological, not sociological, and more narrowly defined in that it concerns the divorce of *foreign* wives and the unprecedented scale of the proceedings. While endogamy, or marriage within the tribe, was clearly the norm in the earlier history of Israel (probably to preserve tribal wealth and land holdings), several notable instances of marriage outside the tribe indicate that Israel did not scrupulously adhere to this norm: for example, Esau's marriage to two Hittites (Gen. 26:34); Joseph's marriage to an Egyptian (Gen. 41:45); Moses' marriage to a Midianite (Exod. 2:21) as well as a Cushite (Num. 12:1); David's marriage to a Calebite and an Aramean (II Sam. 3:3); Solomon's marriages with Pharaoh's daughter, a Moabite, an Ammonite, an Edomite, a Sidonian, and a Hittite (I Kings 11:1; 14:21); as well as Bathsheba's marriage to Uriah the Hittite (II Sam. 11:3) and Hiram's mother's marriage to a Tyrian man (I Kings 7:13f.). On this whole question the reader is referred to D. Bossman's article, "Ezra's Marriage Reform: Israel Redefined."

Furthermore, the book of Ruth, often interpreted as a polemic against Ezra's reform by depicting David as the descendant of a mixed marriage, actually has nothing to say about the fact that this was marriage with a *foreigner* despite seven references to her nationality ("Moabite" 1:22; 2:2, 6, 21; 4:5, 10;

"foreigner" 2:10). Neither are the marriages of Mahlon and Chilion (1:4) condemned, and the near relative does not use Ruth's *foreignness* as a reason for not marrying her (4:6). As long as the foreign partner embraced the faith, there seem to have been no compunctions about the marriage.

What Old Testament prescriptions against intermarriage do exist (e.g., Gen. 28:1, 6; Deut. 7:3–6; Josh. 23:11–13; Judges 3:1–6) seem to have arisen in the period following the fall of the North in 722 B.C. in an effort to counter the religious and political crisis that was crippling the South. This situation is clearly analogous to the one Ezra faced as he sought to implement the stipulations of Artaxerxes's edict to reconstitute Israel as a religious community under the political domination of Persia. This redefinition of Israel's identity demanded a purification of the people on religious grounds. This, in turn, clarifies Ezra's opposition to *foreign* wives. It is not their racial or national ties that are at issue but the religious practices that the foreign wives brought to their marriages and the effects those practices would surely have had upon family and community structures.

When it is remembered that many of the returnees had divorced their Jewish wives in favor of women from the indigenous population (Mal. 2:10–16), Ezra's reforms in this area may be seen, in part, as a correction to an earlier problem of divorce and thus the lesser of two evils.

The church encounters similar situations only in marriages between believers and nonbelievers, and only in individual cases. Here, the warning posed by Ezra and the community must be taken seriously. In the New Testament, however, Paul (and he is careful to say that this is *his* opinion and not necessarily "the Lord's") explicitly forbids divorce as a solution to the problem (I Cor. 7:12f.). Rather, the believing partner is to see the situation as an opportunity for winning the unbelieving partner to the faith.

Distasteful as they may be, the marriage reforms must be seen as a purification of the community along priestly lines of separation from all that was unclean. Their intent was to preserve the faith intact and redefine Israel's identity as a religious community. It must also be remembered that this negative strengthening of the community in the law will be paired with Ezra's positive strengthening of the community in the covenant renewal of Nehemiah 8—10.

Of greater significance for contemporary readers is the message of these chapters regarding the need for continual

57

reformation. From the story of Noah and the flood onward, the Old Testament has unfailingly held before our eyes the inability of humanity, however noble their intentions, however firm their resolve, to maintain the first flush of righteousness that accompanies a really new beginning. In Nehemiah's time, the restoration community would soon find themselves perpetuating the same sin they so vigorously expunged at this juncture. They needed to learn, as did those who experienced God's grace in exodus and wilderness wandering, as do we, that there is no sinless development following deliverance. Rather, sin continues to break out in ever new forms in the new situations created by the God who puts to death the old that God might be brought to life.

Yesterday's gospel becomes today's law, as the Protestant reformers of the sixteenth century tirelessly remind us. The church must always be reformed. The war to end all wars . . . wasn't. But while we may not be able to stand and survey the scene as conquering heroes, we can persevere as warriors in the on-going struggle, confident in the assurance of victory given by the one who has gone before us in death and resurrection.

Return Under Nehemiah and Reconstruction of the Walls

NEHEMIAH 1—4; 6:1—7:3

The books of Ezra and Nehemiah originally comprised a single work. The narrative that begins at Nehemiah 1:1 and continues through 7:3 is, therefore, not a new departure, unrelated to what has gone before, but rather a continuation of the narrative in Ezra. It is, in fact, the third important moment in the history of the restoration as seen through the theological lens of the final editor of these books. As the third moment, this account shares the basic outline of its predecessors (Ezra 1—6; 7—10): a return from Babylon, to undertake a specific project authorized by the Persian crown under the direct influence of God, is met with opposition in Jerusalem. This opposition is

58

countered (again with God's assistance), resulting in the successful completion of the project.

Recognition of this outline confirms the view that Ezra
1:1—Nehemiah 7:3, recounting the parallel returns of Zerubbabel, Ezra, and Nehemiah, forms the first main division of
these books. This emphasis upon continuity with what has
gone before, however, in no way diminishes the lively character of this material, which, as acknowledged by all, springs
from Nehemiah himself complete with asides and personal
reminiscences.

The account is carefully arranged, falling into an extensive
concentric arrangement punctuated by seven similarly introduced episodes of opposition.

The History of Nehemiah (1:1a)
  A Hanani's report, Nehemiah to rebuild city (1:1b—2:8)
    B Letters to governors vouch for Nehemiah (2:9)
      C Opposition (2:10)
        D Inspection by night, Jerusalem: reproach (2:11–18)
          E Opposition, Geshem charges sedition (2:19–20)
            F Wall building (3:1–32)
              G Opposition (4:1)
                H Ridicule (4:2–3)
                  I Prayer (4:4–5)
                    J Wall "joined" to half its height (4:6)
                    J' Opposition "join together" (4:7–8)
                  I' Prayer (4:9)
                H' Ridicule's effect (4:10–14)
              G' Opposition (4:15)
            F' Wall building with defense (4:16–23)

            (Ch. 5: Problems of Nehemiah's second period)

          E' Opposition, Geshem charges sedition (6:1–9)
        D' Nehemiah: threats by night, reproach (6:10–14)
      C' Opposition (6:15–16)
    B' Letters to Tobiah defame Nehemiah (6:17–19)
  A' Hanani placed in charge of rebuilt Jerusalem (7:1–3)

Two matters call for special comment at the beginning: (1)
the thematic importance of the opposition notices, and (2) the
obtrusive nature of chapter 5.

1. Clines (*Ezra, Nehemiah, Esther,* pp. 158, 165), Williamson (*Ezra, Nehemiah,* p. 215), and Blenkinsopp (p. 225), all
following Kellermann, emphasize the fact that every successful

advance in Nehemiah's mission is met with opposition by Sanballat and his associates, introduced by the formula, "When X
heard. . . ." Seven stages are thus presented:

1. 2:10: Sanballat and Tobiah are greatly displeased by *Nehemiah's mission.*
2. 2:19f.: Sanballat, Tobiah, and Geshem mock *the decision
   to rebuild the walls.*
3. 4:1–3: Sanballat and Tobiah, in the presence of the chiefs
   of the Samarian community ("his associates") and the
   Samarian army, mock *Nehemiah's successful organization of the rebuilding.*
4. 4:7f.: Sanballat, Tobiah, the Arabs, the Ammonites, and
   the Ashdodites threaten to fight when *the wall is joined
   to half its height* (4:6).
5. 4:15: "Our enemies" hear that their plot has been frustrated by God; *Judah returns to work on the wall armed
   with sword and trowel.*
6. 6:1–9: Sanballat, Tobiah, Geshem, and the rest of the
   enemies, foiled by *Nehemiah's defense measures*
   (4:9–23), turn to personal attack upon Nehemiah.
7. 6:16: All the enemies realize that the *walls were completed* with divine assistance.

This theme of opposition forms the narrative backbone of
1:1a—7:3. Not only does every stage of the project conclude
with one of these notices, but a gradual intensification within
the notices themselves may also be discerned. This is seen, first
of all, in the swelling coalition of adversaries, from Sanballat and
Tobiah (2:10) through the subsequent additions of Geshem
(2:19), the chiefs of the Samarian community and the Samarian
army (4:2), the Arabs, the Ammonites, and the Ashdodites (4:7),
and "the rest of our enemies" (6:1), to a final collective reference to "all our enemies" in 6:16. From 4:7 on, Israel is surrounded with adversaries from every point on the compass.

The tenor of the opposition becomes increasingly hostile as
well, from the displeasure of 2:10 through the "mockery" and
"ridicule" (both from the same Hebrew term) of 2:19 and 4:1,
to the threat of physical violence (4:8), and malicious personal
attacks upon Nehemiah himself (6:1–9).

60   The presence of prayer in Nehemiah's responses to the
opposition is also noteworthy (2:20; 4:4f., 9; 6:9) and leads to the
interesting observation that in the first and last instances of

opposition, where no response from Nehemiah is recorded, we see a shift in the outlook of the adversaries. In 2:10 they are greatly displeased that a "human being" (*'adam*, not the "someone" in NRSV) had been sent to see to the welfare of the Israelites, while in 6:16 all the enemies were aware that the success of the project was due to the *divine* activity of "our [i.e. Israel's] God."

2. While nobody seriously doubts the authenticity of Nehemiah 5, its present setting in the Nehemiah Memoir is periodically challenged (see, e.g., Michaeli, 1967, pp. 327f.; Ackroyd, *I & II Chronicles, Ezra, Nehemiah,* 1973, p. 281; and most recently, Blenkinsopp, 1988, pp. 255f.). The various reasons for this challenge stem from the observation that the social problems of chapter 5 do not seem to arise out of the difficult situation created by the work on the wall: (1) fifty-two days (6:15) seem too short a period of time for these problems to arise, and Nehemiah 5:14 indicates that a much longer time frame is in view. (2) The text does not attribute the crisis to work on the wall but rather names "famine" (v. 3) as the reason. (3) The wall was finished on Elul 25 (6:15), that is, *before* the time of the olive/grape harvest. On the other hand, Williamson (*Ezra, Nehemiah,* 1985, pp. 255f.) has responded to these persistent charges with plausible explanations of the anomalies just rehearsed.

Two new observations, arising from the structure of the memoir, may be offered as a first step toward a resolution of this stalemate. First, the intricacy of the concentric arrangement of Nehemiah 1:1—7:3, which pairs every major episode in the narrative except chapter 5, suggests the obtrusive nature of Nehemiah's social reforms in this context on structural grounds. Second, as was noted above, the narrative backbone of these chapters concludes the successful completion of each stage in the project with a highly stylized opposition notice. Again, the only exception to this pattern occurs in conjunction with chapter 5, which interrupts the expected connection between 4:23 and 6:1.

If Nehemiah 5 seems obtrusive in its present setting, a number of parallels and formal considerations suggest an original setting following chapter 13. As will be discussed at that point in the commentary, chapter 5, in conjunction with 12:44—13: 14, frames the structurally parallel episodes of 13:15—22 and 13:23—29.

61

With the omission of chapter 5, then, these chapters fall into three sections, each of which describes the ever-narrowing reproach of the community at the hands of the opposition, first with regard to Jerusalem (1:1—2:20), then the builders (3:1—4:23), and finally Nehemiah himself (6:1—7:3).

Nehemiah 1—2
Jerusalem as Reproach

These chapters mark the beginning of the so-called Nehemiah Memoir, which extends through 7:3. They announce the main themes and introduce us to the main characters of that narrative: Nehemiah, Artaxerxes, Sanballat, Tobiah, and Geshem, the Israelite community, and, of course, God. Following the superscription, "The words [or "deeds"] of Nehemiah son of Hacaliah" (1:1a), the narrative is carefully structured in five sections whose main theme is to record four reports of the destruction of Jerusalem as a reproach against God and the various responses made to those reports (1:1b–11a; 1:11b—2:8; 2:11–16 and 2:17–20). The center section (2:9–10) introduces the theme of opposition that will carry the remainder of the narrative.

> A   Report to Nehemiah and response (1:1b–11a)
> B   Report to Artaxerxes and response (1:11b—2:8)
> X   Opposition (2:9–10)
> B′   Report: Nehemiah sees for himself (2:11–16)
> A′   Report to leaders and response (2:17–20)

The NRSV has obscured the close wording of the destruction reports in 1:3; 2:3, 13, 17. Both 1:3 and 2:17 (A, A′) contain identical descriptions in Hebrew, "and her gates were *burned* by fire," as do 2:3 and 13 (B, B′) "and her gates were *consumed* by fire." Further terminological linking of A and A′ is indicated by the repetition of "God of heaven" (1:4f. and 2:20); "your/his servants" (1:6, 10, and 2:20); and "give success" (1:11a and 2:20). The concept of the survivors being "in shame" (1:3) and "disgrace" (2:17) reflects the same Hebrew term, "reproach" *(herpah)*, and forms an inclusion for the entire passage.

In addition to the concentric structure just presented, we also observe that the narrative is shaped to mark Nehemiah's

62

progress from Susa, the winter residence of the Persian kings and the setting of 1:1—2:8 (A, B), through the province of Beyond the River, the setting of 2:9–10 (X), to Jerusalem, the setting of the remainder of his work and where he carries out his initial approach to the problem of the walls, 2:11–20 (B', A'). These transitions are marked in the text by the repetition of "Then/So I came to X" at 2:9, 11.

This structural analysis has lifted up the theme of Jerusalem's destruction as a reproach against God. The fourfold repetition of the report of that destruction in Nehemiah's encounters with God, Artaxerxes, the destruction itself, and the community, as well as the subsequent responses emerging from those encounters will serve to organize the exposition of the passage.

Encounter with God: Nehemiah's Faith (1:1b–11a)

The opening verse presents a difficult historical problem. Who is the king Nehemiah serves and what year provides the setting for this passage? There is a wide consensus, based on evidence in the Elephantine papyri, that Artaxerxes I (465–424) is the king in question. Much less agreement is found respecting the date of Nehemiah's conversations, due to the apparent discrepancy between 1:1, which mentions the *ninth* month, Chislev, and 2:1, which speaks of Nisan, the *first* month of the Jewish calendar. Attractive solutions are that we either read "nineteenth year" at 1:1 (Biblia Hebraica Stuttgartensia) or assume Nehemiah is here reckoning the twentieth year as the *regnal* year of Artaxerxes, 446 (Bickerman). Of primary importance for our purposes is the four-month gap between Nehemiah's hearing of the destruction of Jerusalem and his encounter with the king.

Theologically speaking, it is important to realize that the bulk of the passage records Nehemiah's *second* response to the devastating news from Jerusalem. Following a period of grief (1:4, cf. Ezra 9:3–5), his initial response, Nehemiah demonstrates his faith by turning to the fount of his resources in prayer. While the form of the prayer itself is unparalleled in scripture—it lacks, for instance, the complaint so characteristic of the community laments with which it is sometimes compared (Williamson, *Ezra, Nehemiah*, p. 167)—it falls easily into a simple structure:

63

INTERPRETATION

    A   Invocation (5–6a)
     B   Confession: Israel's sin (6b–7)
      X   Appeal to covenantal promise of return (8–9)
     B' Confession: God's redemption (10)
    A' Invocation with supplication (11a)

The prayer begins and ends with an invocation similar to that found in Solomon's prayer at the dedication of the temple (I Kings 8:29, 52; II Chron. 6:40), "let your ear be attentive . . . to hear the prayer of your servant" (6a, 11a). Two confessions, one negative, regarding Israel's sin (B), and one positive, regarding God's redemption (B'), frame the heart of the prayer (X). This centerpiece consists of Nehemiah's appeal to God to remember the covenantal promise of return on the basis of Deuteronomy 30:1–5. The strengthened particle of entreaty with the vocative, "O LORD" (5, 11a), provide an inclusion for the entire prayer.

The opening verses of invocation are important for their emphasis upon the power of God, especially as Nehemiah here uses the title "God of heaven," which became increasingly more common in postexilic piety (e.g. Jonah 1:9; Dan. 2:37–44). A clue to the interpretation of the entire prayer is also hinted at in the invocation. Whereas the delegation from Jerusalem contented itself with the reporting of the city's reproach in the eyes of jealous neighbors, Nehemiah discerns the true source of the problem: Israel's failure with regard to the covenant. His invocation of the God "who keeps covenant and steadfast love" (1:5) displays a keen insight into the reason for Jerusalem's reproach as well as the relationship of God to the sorry condition of the city.

This insight moves Nehemiah to confess the sin of his people. In the tradition of past mediators (Moses, Exod. 34:9; Isaiah, Isa. 6:5; Ezra, Ezra 9; cf. Daniel, Dan. 9:3–19), Nehemiah confesses his own involvement in the sin of the people, thus identifying with their condition and situation (1:6). The exile proved to be an effective if harsh lesson for the people of God. Jeremiah's understanding of the captivity as a manifestation of God's chastisement was met with beatings and imprisonment (Jeremiah 18—20), but now the exiles were fully convinced of the truth of his warnings. Consequently, Nehemiah refuses to pass the blame on to others or to complain about the disastrous situation in Jerusalem but simply acknowledges their guilt.

This aspect of the confession is quite different from Ezra's earlier confession (Ezra 9:6–15). There, though Ezra begins with an acknowledgment of the people's sin as the reason for the exile (v. 7), he quickly moves to the confession of a specific sin that he did not share, that of intermarriage. Nehemiah seems to be more concerned with the sinful condition of his people than with symptomatic outcroppings. This sinful condition he confesses simply and succinctly as sins "against you."

A simplistic understanding of the covenant as a pact that somehow obligates God to dispense forgiveness so long as Israel keeps covenant obviously will not do, if for no other reason than that Nehemiah has just confessed Israel's failure in this regard. But a more theologically astute understanding that would allow the covenant people to demand forgiveness on the basis of God's promise also seriously misreads the situation. The covenant does not set up a business transaction between two parties. In its essence, the covenant establishes a relationship. More importantly, the covenant does not dispense with the need for mercy, indeed the covenant itself grows out of God's mercy, grace, and steadfast love. Covenant and mercy go hand in hand, and our need of mercy is in no way obviated by a contractual arrangement. Nehemiah's confession is an appeal to God's mercy.

The heart of the prayer is also its turning point (vv. 8–9). Nehemiah reminds God that the lesson has been learned; the exiles have been scattered among the peoples for their unfaithfulness. This is to be seen as a testimony to God's power and control of history. Israel is in God's hands, not subject to the capricious machinations of human despots. Therefore, God's judgment upon Israel's sin, related in the summary of Deuteronomy 30:1–5 in Nehemiah 1:8, has been carried out. But as the positive confession of verse 10 intimates ("your servants") and verse 11a declares ("your servants who delight in revering your name"), the signs of repentance are present as well, and so Nehemiah appeals to God to remember the promise of return also contained in Deuteronomy 30:1–5 (1:9).

It is best to see the prayer to this point as a summary of Nehemiah's struggles with God over the four-month gap between his conversation with the delegation from Jerusalem and his audience with Artaxerxes. His final petition, however, looks forward to the events of 2:1–8. Here, realizing that he will be

God's instrument, he prays for success with his capricious master (1:11a).

This calls attention to another progression in the organization of the prayer. Nehemiah begins with contemplation of God; only then does he move to the contemplation of human sin. This gradual narrowing of the prayer from the divine to the human continues as he turns his attention first to the concerns of the people and only at the end to his personal situation. As the prayer becomes more specific, we are directed to the crucial nature of the encounter to which we now turn.

Encounter with Artaxerxes: Nehemiah's Courage (1:11b—2:8)

The circumstantial clause in 1:11b, "At that time, I was cupbearer to the king," has received a great deal of attention in the literature. The Greek tradition offers two separate renderings, "cupbearer" *(oinochoos)* and "eunuch" *(eunouchos)*. Some have used this Greek variant to explain the repeated emphasis on "remember me, O my God" (5:19; 13:14, 22, 31) in the Nehemiah Memoir. If Nehemiah were a eunuch, he would not have any offspring to preserve his memory in the traditional Old Testament way. The Nehemiah Memoir would thus serve as his memorial. Recent interpreters, however, are wisely suspicious of what looks to be a scribal error for "cupbearer" in the Greek tradition.

A more satisfactory interpretation sees this last clause of 1:11 as a transition between 1:1–11a and 2:1–8. No menial servants, royal cupbearers were charged with tasting the king's wine (to prevent poisoning) and guarding the royal chambers. As such they became among the most trusted of officials and throughout the Near East enjoyed extensive influence with their masters. In Nehemiah's case, the office also provided an opportunity to plead his case.

At this point another vexing historical question asserts itself. Nehemiah can hardly have been surprised and distressed at Hanani's report of the sorry state of Jerusalem if that report refers to the destruction of the city by Nebuchadnezzar in 587. One of the results of that siege was the very existence of Nehemiah's Jewish colony in Babylon. Rather, we must look to the events resulting from the correspondence in Ezra 4:7–23 and

66

dated in the reign of Artaxerxes I. The destruction reported to Nehemiah must have taken place sometime after Ezra's mission in the seventh year of that reign and before the delegation headed by Hanani came to Susa. This reconstruction would fully account for Nehemiah's surprise and distress in that he would immediately realize that his Persian master was responsible for the condition of Jerusalem and its inhabitants.

It also provides us with another glimpse into the character of Nehemiah, whose presence will dominate the next six chapters. Here Nehemiah's courage is highlighted. No feats of bravery would be required had the destruction been at the hands of Babylon. Babylon lay defeated. But if the more recent events recounted in Ezra 4:23 lie behind Hanani's report, then the work Nehemiah was to undertake had been attempted less than thirteen years before with disastrous results, including the arousal of jealousy among the surrounding peoples and sanctions imposed by Nehemiah's master.

The one ray of hope to be seen in all this is the somewhat capricious nature of Artaxerxes, who seems to fluctuate between favorable attitudes toward Jerusalem, as indicated in the commissioning of Ezra, and more negative ones, as seen in the devastating decree of Ezra 4:21. Yet even here we note the tempering effect of an "escape clause": "Therefore issue an order that these people be made to cease, and that this city not be rebuilt, *until I make a decree.*" Planting the seed of such a reversal will call upon all of Nehemiah's courage and resources.

The passage is structured as a series of three exchanges between Artaxerxes and Nehemiah (2:2f.; 4f.; 6–8a). In each exchange a question by Artaxerxes (2:2a; 4a; 6a) is followed by a reaction from Nehemiah (fear, 2:2b; prayer, 4b; proposed length of stay, 6b) and a speech introduced by, "Then I said to the king . . ." (2:3; 5; 7–8a). This dialogical material is enclosed in a narrative frame that speaks of Nehemiah "giving" *(natan)* wine to the king (2:1) and the king "granting" *(natan)* Nehemiah's request (2:8b).

Most of the information here is already familiar from the previous destruction report. Consequently, the text focuses on the individuals involved. Artaxerxes is depicted as interested and concerned about his court favorite, direct and probing in his questioning, and pleased to grant every request. Nehemiah, *externally,* displays proper respect and attention to court eti-

67

quette in his responses to the king. But as the structure of the passage makes clear, we can observe an *internal* growth in confidence as Nehemiah becomes increasingly assured that God has answered his four-month period of prayer affirmatively. The first exchange reveals Nehemiah's apprehension at Artaxerxes's innocent inquiry as to his well-being: "I was very much afraid" (v. 2b). His fear stems from uncertainty now that the time had come, especially since his request would in fact require a change in imperial policy. Nevertheless, he launches into a description of the sorry state of "the city, the place of my ancestors' graves" (v. 3). This second destruction report sets the stage for Artaxerxes's response.

The second exchange marks the turning point. Artaxerxes still controls the situation with his question, "What do you request?" (v. 4a), but Nehemiah's reaction, "So I prayed to the God of heaven" (v. 4b), reminds the reader of the presence of a third party, who will remain behind the scenes throughout the narrative.

The expositor might decide to compare the interrelatedness of the long prayer of 1:4–11a and this short petition offered at the moment of crisis. Both spring from Nehemiah's closeness to God and dependence on divine support. Both have a role to play in the life of the believer, much as the long high priestly prayer of Jesus in John 17 compares and contrasts with the short cry of dereliction on the cross or the prayer in the Garden. Nehemiah's turning to God as the source of strength in all aspects of life is one of his most attractive qualities.

Nehemiah, in his growing confidence, asks to be sent home to rebuild the city (v. 5). Much has been made of Nehemiah's care to avoid the name of "the city, the place of my ancestors' graves." Whether we see diplomacy here or simply Nehemiah's casting of the request as a personal tragedy, it is clear that Artaxerxes would have been aware that Jerusalem was the intended destination.

If the chronology we have adopted is accurate, there is some evidence that Artaxerxes would have been only too willing to fortify Jerusalem as a much-needed buffer against the rebellions of Egypt and the province of Beyond the River. These had increased in intensity throughout this part of his reign. In this case, Nehemiah's diplomatic skill would be tested to the utmost since Jerusalem had been implicated in such rebellions previously (Ezra 4:12–16). Yet the text refuses to assign a political motivation to what is presented as a direct consequence of the royal favor.

The third exchange begins with a tacit granting of Nehemiah's request, "How long will you be gone, and when will you return?" (v. 6). Nehemiah's confidence is complete, and he responds without mention of fear or prayer. In his subsequent speech he details further requests for the success of the project: letters of introduction to the governors of the province Beyond the River for safe conduct through their jurisdiction and to the king's chief forester Asaph, for the timber required by the three main building projects: the gates, the wall, and his own residence (v. 7–8). These details suggest that Nehemiah's last four months had been spent in careful planning as well as prayer.

The closing lines of this section are important for the balance they suggest between the human and divine sources of power that will drive the project through to its successful completion. It is clearly stated that Artaxerxes granted Nehemiah all that he requested, and Nehemiah had obviously devoted many long hours in careful preparation and prayer; yet the reason for the granting of the requests is neither royal favor nor faithful preparation. In a phrase reminiscent of Ezra's mission (Ezra 7:6, 9, 28; 8:18, 22, 31; cf. Neh. 2:18) Nehemiah ascribes the success of his conversations with Artaxerxes to the gracious power of God (2:8b).

Opposition (2:9–10)

In terms of the travel theme of 1:1b—2:20, these two verses serve as a transition between the settings of Susa and Jerusalem. Their central position in this context, however, indicates that their significance is not exhausted by this simple observation. Three issues call for comment.

First, it is striking that the description of the journey is so briefly recounted. The only points related are the presentation of the royal letters of introduction and a notice that Nehemiah, unlike Ezra (Ezra 8:22), accepted a military escort. Kidner may be right in claiming more for the escort than protection. Such an arrival in style would impressively reinforce Nehemiah's credentials to skeptical neighboring governors and underline the change in royal policy (p. 81).

While our knowledge of these governors is modest, we do have some extrabiblical information. The Elephantine papyri

69

refer to Sanballat as "governor of Samaria" in 407 B.C., some thirty-eight years after the time of our text. The names of his sons, Delaiah and Shelemaiah, which are compounded with a shortened version of "Yahweh," have been seen as evidence that Sanballat was at least a nominal Yahwist. The marriage of his daughter to a member of the high priestly family (13:28) may further substantiate this impression.

Even less is known of Tobiah, usually thought to have been the Persian governor of Ammon. Several attempts have been made to link Tobiah with the powerful Moabite family of the same name, but it is more likely that this common name (also a compound of "Yahweh," as is the name of his son, "Jehohanan" [6:18]) refers to a Samarian official subordinate in some way to Sanballat.

A second issue concerns the introduction of the theme of opposition in verse 10. As presented in the introduction to this section, the alternation between successful completion of one stage of the operation and renewed opposition forms the narrative backbone of Nehemiah 1—7.

Finally, J. G. McConville (*Ezra, Nehemiah and Esther*, p. 82) has drawn attention to the central importance of these verses for the interpretation of 1:1—2:20. Though not immediately obvious in the NRSV, the contrast between good *(tob)* and evil *(ra')* is pervasive. The "trouble" of Jerusalem in 1:3 and 2:17 is literally "evil," as is Nehemiah's "sadness" in 2:1–3. On the other hand, the expressions "it *pleased* the king" (2:6, cf. v. 7), "the *gracious* hand of God" upon Nehemiah (2:8, cf. v. 18), and "the common *good*" (2:18), that is, the reconstruction of the walls, all employ various nuances of the adjective "good." The theme reaches a pointed climax in 2:10 where Sanballat and Tobiah, governors in Beyond the River, are greatly "displeased" *(ra')* "that someone ["some human," *'adam*] had come to seek the welfare [*tob*] of the people of Israel."

The stage is thus set for depicting Nehemiah's mission as a conflict between good and evil. Those elements that foster the success of the mission, whether human (the king) or divine (God's "hand" or power) are designated "good," while those elements that seek to impede the mission or arise from the present situation (Nehemiah's grief, Jerusalem's plight, and the reaction of Sanballat and Tobiah) are seen to be "evil." With the stage thus set, the narrative is free to begin the account of the wall building.

Encounter with Reality:
Nehemiah's Night Ride (2:11–16)

This interpretation has stressed the importance of the four destruction reports in 1:3; 2:3, 13, 17, for the structure and exposition of Nehemiah 1 and 2. The interpretation of the present passage is especially well-served in this regard. Typical expositions emphasize the historical value of verses 13–15 for the topographical understanding of Jerusalem they provide, but one need only compare the numerous charts and conflicting representations of the city as it was supposed to have been in Nehemiah's time to realize the scanty nature of this information as we now have it. One point, that the city did *not* include the Western hill (Williamson, *PEQ*, pp. 81–88), is fairly certain now and will be assumed in the discussion of chapters 3 and 12. Close examination of the structure and attention to the presence of a destruction report, however, point to a different expository approach for these verses.

Nehemiah's "Night Ride" is somewhat loosely organized around a number of repetitions:

A   "I told no one" (11–12)
  B   "I went out by the Valley Gate" (13a)
    X   "I inspected the wall(s)" (13b–15a)
  B'   "I entered by the Valley Gate" (15b)
A'   "I had not yet told the Jews . . ." (16)

The outer elements share references to "not telling" as well as "to do," while the inner elements serve as the beginning and end of the journey as Nehemiah goes out and then reenters by means of the "Valley Gate." The center of the passage contains a double reference to Nehemiah's primary activity of "inspecting the wall(s)" (vv. 13b, 15a), which frames the third of the four destruction reports. It must be admitted that the terminology "destruction *report*" is less apt here since it is Nehemiah's personal investigation of the wall that is narrated. Nevertheless, the importance of this firsthand confirmation of earlier reports (1:3; 2:3) should not be overlooked.

This may be seen in two ways: (1) As a shrewd and practical administrator, Nehemiah realized the folly of attempting to involve the local authorities before he himself was aware of the

71

exact nature of the situation. A prematurely formulated plan that would aggravate the already smoldering animosity of Jerusalem's neighbors stood little chance of winning the approval of the inhabitants. Not only must he be able to offer a clear and definite proposal, he must also convince them that he understood the complexities of the situation. Thus, the destruction report, framed by the double mention of Nehemiah's personal investigation of the walls, confirms Hanani's report at Susa (1:3).

(2) Quite apart from this practical consideration is one of motivation. We all share a tendency to be more moved by tragedy that we have seen or experienced ourselves than tragedy that we have only heard about. Nehemiah had "mourned for days" (1:4) upon hearing the first report of Jerusalem's destruction. We can only imagine the impact that seeing the demolished walls with his own eyes had upon him. And yet the text is completely silent on this point. There is no mention of grief, weeping, fasting, lamentation, or despair here or in the rest of the memoir. What we do see, in verses 17–20, is the beginning of Nehemiah's decisive action to remedy the situation.

Encounter with the People: Nehemiah's Diplomacy (2:17–20)

This last part of the introductory section of the memoir presents Nehemiah's report of the destruction and his appeal to the inhabitants of Jerusalem to rebuild the walls. Their response and the reaction of the opposition are also recounted. As the following diagram shows, the passage is structured around three occurrences of the phrase "let us/we will (arise) and build," which occur at the outer extremes and in the center (2:17, 18b, 20). Framing the people's response is Nehemiah's rationale and the questioning of his rationale by Sanballat, Tobiah, and now Geshem the Arab, who, according to extrabiblical sources, controlled areas to the east and south of Israel (Moab, Edom, and portions of Arabia). Geshem's significance with respect to Nehemiah lies in his geographical location. With the addition of Geshem, the south is included in the opposition, thereby closing the ring around Jerusalem. Furthermore, the structural connection between Geshem and the mention of "rebellion" (2:19, 6:6) reminds us of the success this accusation previously enjoyed with the same Persian king (Ezra 4:7–22).

A   Nehemiah's report and appeal: "Let us rebuild" (17)
  B   Rationale: God's good hand and king's word (18a)
    X   People's response: "Let us start building" (18b)
  B' Rationale attacked: "Rebelling against the king?" (19)
A' Nehemiah's retort: "The God of heaven . . . will give us success, and we his servants are going to start building" (20)

The question of God's role in the project immediately presents itself as the issue. Throughout these initial chapters Nehemiah has consistently attributed his success to the direct intervention of God (1:11; 2:4, 8, 12, 18, 20). While he mentions the royal decree in his rationale of the program to the inhabitants of Jerusalem (though even that political justification springs from God's prompting, 2:8), one might assume that his listeners were swayed by his testimony to the presence of God in his activities, especially as this is given pride of place (2:18a). This assurance of divine assistance, coupled with Nehemiah's sensitive use of the first person plural ("let *us* rebuild . . . that *we* may no longer suffer disgrace," v. 17), by which he subtly affirms his solidarity with them, accounts for the positive response of the people.

As we saw in the discussion at 2:9–10 dealing with the theme of opposition in general, however, the basic error of Sanballat and his associates is one of consistently leaving God out of the discussion and concentrating on the political aspects of the project. That basic mistake is continued at this juncture. In their attack on Nehemiah's rationale, they totally ignore the divine justification for the work and attempt to impeach Nehemiah's testimony regarding the royal decree. The question "What is this that you are doing?" (2:19) is a standardized formula for making an accusation (cf. H. J. Boecker, pp. 25–34).

But Nehemiah will not be swayed. He calmly reasserts the theological warrant for the work, this time without reference to the king (v. 20). The authority of God over against human or political power is a theme that runs through these books and that remains as relevant today as it was in the period of the restoration. In these first two chapters Nehemiah has displayed

73

an appropriate appreciation of the power structures that obtain. His first encounter was with God, followed by an encounter with the king. Only after surveying the situation itself did he approach the community with a well-thought-out plan for the diplomatic alleviation of the problem.

The section concludes with the cryptic "but you have no share or claim or historic right in Jerusalem" (v. 20b). Whether we decide the three terms to have reference to "civil, legal, and cultic rights in the Jerusalem community" (Williamson, *Ezra, Nehemiah,* p. 193) or "the past, present, and future of these unenviable outsiders," as Kidner trenchantly observes (p. 84), the battle lines have been drawn and the opening salvos fired.

Nehemiah 3—4
Narrowing Reproach:
The Builders, Repair, and Defense

We have seen that the Nehemiah Memoir falls into three sections, each of which describes the ever-narrowing reproach of the community at the hands of the opposition. Taken together, the two chapters that comprise this second section relate all but the completion of the building activity undertaken in the restoration of the walls. As in chapter 6, the narrative also describes the opposition of the surrounding peoples and Nehemiah's considerable skill in countering their attempts to thwart the project. Despite this clear narrative flow, however, few commentators examine these chapters together. The major obstacle to the unity of the section lies in the character of the list of those engaged in rebuilding the wall (3:1–32), which diverges from the rest of the Nehemiah Memoir in at least four ways.

1. The repeated notice that the builders "set up its doors, its bolts, and its bars" (vv. 3, 6, 13, 14, 15; cf. v. 1) is at odds with Nehemiah's statement later in the memoir that "up to that time I had not set up the doors in the gates" (6:1).

2. Contrary to Nehemiah's first-person prose, the account is entirely in the third person.

3. The Hebrew word translated "nobles" in verse 5 differs

74

from Nehemiah's regular terminology in the rest of the memoir (2:16; 5:7; 6:17; 7:5; 13:17).

4. Also in verse 5, the probable reference to Nehemiah as "their lord" (despite NRSV "their Lord" or "their lords," mg.) is unusual.

This evidence convincingly argues for the independent origin of the list, possibly from material in the Temple archives, since Eliashib, the high priest, figures prominently. The question is, did Nehemiah appropriate the list for use in his memoir (e.g., Kellermann, pp. 14–17), or was it added later by a subsequent redactor or compiler (e.g., Mowinckel, pp. 109–116)? With the majority of recent scholars, we will assume the former to be the case (cf. the useful summary of opinion in Williamson, *Ezra, Nehemiah*, pp. 200–202).

The section, however, displays an overall coherence that has not generally been recognized, even by those who affirm Nehemiah's use of the previously independent list of builders in his memoir. Careful attention to the repetition of key words throughout the passage supports the following narrative structure:

A   Wall building: "repaired" *(ḥzq)* (3:1–32)
　B   Opposition: "When X heard . . ." (4:1)
　　C   Reproach: "Jews" "rubbish" (4:2–3)
　　　D   Prayer: "our God" (4:4–5)
　　　　E   Wall half completed: "joined together" *(qšr)* (4:6)
　　　　E′   Opposition: "plotted together" *(qšr)* (4:7–8)
　　　D′   Prayer: "our God" (4:9)
　　C′   Effect of reproach upon Jews: "rubbish" "Jews" (4:10–14)
　B′   Opposition: "When X heard . . ." (4:15)
A′   Wall building and defense: "held" *(ḥzq)* weapon (4:16–23)

The pronounced repetition of "repaired" *(ḥzq)* throughout chapter 3 (34 times in Hebrew, only lacking in vv. 1–3 and 25–26; the NRSV and RSV rightly restore "repaired" in vv. 25–26) establishes it as the key word for this first paragraph (A). The triple occurrence of the participial form of this same root in the last paragraph (4:16, 17, 21) with the meaning "held" his weapon is a wordplay that effectively ties the two descriptions

75

of the wall building together and provides an inclusion for the section that emphasizes its two themes: repair and defense. Paragraphs B, B', and E' share the familiar opposition formula "When X heard . . ." (4:1, 7, 15). The ridicule and reproach of the opposition (C, vv. 2–3) and the subsequent report of its demoralizing effect on the workers (C', vv. 10–14) share references to "rubbish" (vv. 2, 10) and "the Jews" (vv. 2, 12).

Two prayers to "our God" (vv. 4, 9), one recorded (D, vv. 4–5) and one narrated (D', v. 9), frame the crucial center of the passage. Here, the midpoint of the memoir as well as the project is reached with the tersely worded, "So we rebuilt the wall, and all the wall was joined together to half its height" (E, v. 6). Following this significant advance in the status of the project comes the expected opposition notice (E', vv. 7–8). These central elements are linked by yet another wordplay, this time on the root *qšr*. In verse 6 the rare niphal stem (I Sam. 18:1 is the only other occurrence) is used of the wall being "joined together," while in verse 8 the more common qal stem describes the "plotting together" of the opposition.

The significance of this ordering of the material lies in its demonstration of the coherence of chapters 3 and 4. Chapter 3 is shown to have a necessary function in the memoir as it stands, quite apart from its original setting, and in conjunction with chapter 4 displays a dual thematic purpose for this section: repair and defense, as suggested by the striking wordplay on *ḥzq*. Following a brief discussion of the historical detail here presented, this dual thematic purpose will be explored.

It is easy to lose sight of the key theological issues of these chapters amid the mass of detail. Yet the detail provides tantalizingly meager information. About all we can say with certainty is that the description begins and ends near the northeast corner of the wall at the Sheep Gate (3:1, 32) and moves around the perimeter of the city in a counterclockwise fashion, as had Nehemiah's earlier "Night Ride" (2:13–15). Through verse 15, the rebuilding follows the old wall of the city, restoring the six gates mentioned in verses 1, 3, 6, 13, 14, and 15, and the connecting sections of wall between them. From verse 16 to the end, however, the building activity follows a new line, farther up the slope, on the eastern side of the City of David (the old Jebusite city) overlooking the Kidron Valley.

The topographical features mentioned in this section are not part of the wall itself but are intended as reference points.

Unfortunately, most of these cannot be defined with any certainty. Williamson suggests such a reconstruction may explain the curious terminological shift between 3:1–15, where the transitions between builders are marked by the phrase "next to him/them," and 3:16–32, where these transitions are indicated by the phrase "after him/them" (*Ezra, Nehemiah*, p. 200). Rudolph (p. 115) draws our attention to five Persian administrative centers that may be implied by the use of the word "ruler" (though we might add that usually this occurs in a phrase, "ruler of [half] the district of X"): Jerusalem (vv. 9, 12), Beth-haccherem (v. 14), Mizpah (vv. 15, 19), Beth-zur (v. 16), and Keilah (vv. 17–18).

Two themes for exposition thus present themselves: repair of the walls, as seen in the list of builders (3:1–32), and defense of the city against opposition, as seen in the events of chapter 4.

Repair of the Walls (Nehemiah 3)

We have seen elsewhere that the lists in Ezra–Nehemiah, while originally intended to catalog information of a more or less historical nature, function theologically in their present settings, usually as a representation of the community's political and cultic status as they move toward their new standing as the reconstituted people of God. Here the emphasis is clearly on the unity of the people.

This is indicated in the careful wording of 3:1–3. In the previous chapter the people had responded to Nehemiah's exhortation to rebuild the walls with a ringing, "Let us start building" (2:18, literally: "Let us *rise up* and *build*"), a phrase that provided the basic structure of the passage (cf. 2:17, 18, 20). The first fruits of these intentions are realized when "the high priest Eliashib set to work [literally: *"rose up,"* RSV] with his fellow priests and *rebuilt* the Sheep Gate" (3:1). After forging this connecting link with chapter 2, the list settles into its characteristic terminology for building, "repaired" (vv. 4–32), the frequent repetition of which has the effect of stressing the solidarity of the community as they work together on the difficult task.

But within this unity of purpose there is room for diversity. The variety of builders working side-by-side is striking. Sometimes they are identified by family, other times by profession or place of residence. Some were priests, others were lay people. Some were rulers of districts, others were merchants. In general terms one could say the broad spectrum of the fledgling community was well-represented in this list so that all took part in the common task before them.

Nehemiah seems to have organized the builders in such a way that, as far as possible, each would be responsible for the part of the wall that lay opposite his own house. This eliminated arguments as to who would work where and motivated the workers to make that part of the wall that defended them as secure as possible. Even in those cases where this would clearly be impossible (e.g. those workers identified as inhabitants of neighboring towns, vv. 2, 5, 7, 14–17), Nehemiah's intention to unify the people shines through. Just as Josiah had found cultic centralization at Jerusalem the best means of establishing unity in worship (II Kings 23), Nehemiah was convinced of the necessity of participation by those living in the outlying areas to cement their political ties with the Holy City.

In rebuilding the city walls, then, Nehemiah was doing much more than providing for the defense of the community. He was also restoring its essential unity. The rebuilding was to have further consequences with regard to another problem of the restoration, intermarriage. One can hardly deny that the defenseless state of the city prior to Nehemiah's arrival aggravated the difficulties involved in keeping the community separate from the surrounding peoples and contributed to the aristocracy's encouragement of intermarriage. After the city had been made secure and had been repopulated, the fortifications of the city would go a long way toward maintaining that separateness of identity that was so important in this period.

Defense of the City (Nehemiah 4)

When we turn to the events of chapter 4, dealing with the defense of the city against opposition, the appropriateness of two of Nehemiah's tactics comes into question. As we saw in the discussion of structure, this chapter falls into two panels, 4:1–6 and 4:7–23. Verses 1–6 may be seen as setting the stage. Verses 1–3 begin with the formula of opposition that forms the narrative backbone of the Nehemiah Memoir, "Now when Sanballat heard . . ." (v. 1), and they expand into a taunting reproach of the builders by means of five rhetorical questions designed to undermine their confidence (v. 2). Sanballat is joined in his ridicule by Tobiah the Ammonite in verse 3. Verses 4–5 present Nehemiah's response in the form of a prayer of imprecation, followed by a statement in verse 6 testifying to the persever- ance of the Jews that marks the midpoint of the Nehemiah Memoir: "So we rebuilt the wall, and all the wall was joined together to half its height; for the people had a mind to work."

The rest of the chapter can be seen as an expanded repeti- tion of this basic pattern infused with imagery from the holy war traditions of ancient Israel. Kellermann has catalogued the various connections between verses 7–23 and these early tradi- tions (p. 18):

1. The enemies band together intending "to fight" against Israel (vv. 7–8).
2. The people call upon God for help before arming them- selves (v. 9).
3. Mention is made of the extremely limited nature of the defensive capabilities of the people (vv. 10, 13).
4. The Jewish forces are a drafted militia arranged by fam- ily (v. 13).
5. The leader declares holy war ("Our God will fight for us," v. 20b) and in an address summons the people to courage and faithfulness ("Do not be afraid of them. Remember the Lord," v. 14).
6. The Lord frustrates the intentions of the enemies, whose courage fails them (v. 15).
7. Trumpets are employed in battle summons (vv. 18–19).

As in verses 1–6, verses 7–8 repeat the opposition formula and verse 9 presents the Jewish response in the form of a nar- rated prayer. Unlike verses 1–6, however, this panel does not end with a statement testifying to the perseverance of the Jews. Rather the ridicule and reproach of verses 2–3, supposedly neu- tralized after Nehemiah's imprecation, seem to have had an effect after all, and a demoralizing one at that, as seen in verses 10–12. Much of the expansion and certainly the postponement of the denouement in these verses can be attributed to the addition of the holy war materials. Again, attention to the repe- tition of phrases and words helps in the discernment of the following structure:

79

INTERPRETATION

    A Jerusalem threatened with war (7–9)
      B People fear they will not be able to work (10–12)
        C Encouragement to nobles, officials, and people (13–14)
          X God frustrates enemies: sword and trowel defense (15–18)
        C' Encouragement to nobles, officials, and people (19–20)
      B' People labor at the work (21)
    A' Jerusalem defended (22–23)

Mention of "Jerusalem," "guard," "day," and "night" links verses 7–9 with 22–23 (A, A'). The contrast between the people's inability to work on the wall in verses 10–12 and the statement "So we labored at the work" in verse 21, links B and B', as does the emphatic positioning of "we" at the head of a clause (vv. 10, 21). Framing the central assertion that God had frustrated the plans of the enemies (crucial for the holy war traditions) and the description of the so-called "sword and trowel" defensive measures of the community in verses 15–18, is a brace of encouraging speeches made by Nehemiah "to the nobles and to the officials and to the rest of the people" (vv. 14, 19), which function together as the prebattle exhortation of the holy war traditions.

THEOLOGICAL IMPLICATIONS

The difficulty this material presents for contemporary readers lies in the two responses made to the opposition's taunts and threats: Nehemiah's imprecatory prayer in verses 4–5, and the holy war posturing that dominates verses 7–23.

As we look at Nehemiah's prayer, once again we encounter the term "reproach" *(herpah)*, here translated "taunt" (4:4). As we have seen, this key word dominates the Nehemiah Memoir. Nehemiah uses this term in chapters 1 and 2 to describe the sorry state of Jerusalem and its inhabitants (1:3; 2:17). In chapter 6 we will see how the enemies' attack is directed against Nehemiah himself (6:13). The present passage stands between these two as a transition in the narrowing progression of reproach. Here the builders are singled out for defamation (4:4). Particular nuance is given to the term through a clever wordplay: By asking Yahweh to deliver Sanballat and his associates into the hands of their enemies that they might become "plunder" *(biz-*

zah), Nehemiah seeks a reversal of the builders' "despised" *(buzah)* condition. The answer to this prayer is recorded in 6:16.

Actually, Nehemiah's prayer has much in common with the psalms of imprecation (e.g., Ps. 35:4–6; 58:6–9; 59:11–15; 69:22–28; 83:9–17; 109:6–19; 137:7–9; helpful discussions of the pastoral implications of these psalms may be found in C. S. Lewis, *Reflections on the Psalms,* pp. 20–33, and W. Brueggemann's discussion of Psalm 109 in *The Message of the Psalms,* pp. 81–88). These "cursing psalms" are best understood as an expansion of the element of petition in the laments. Usually, the psalmist limits himself to a plea for deliverance from the previously related description of distress. In the imprecatory psalms, however, a second petition is offered: not only "Save me!" but "Get them!" That these unsavory requests are not merely spur-of-the-moment sentiments is revealed in the careful poetic and literary language and style in which they are couched. The psalmists obviously invested a great deal of time, energy, and thought in their invective.

Understandably, the church has been troubled by these passages. Marcion was appalled by these cries for vengeance and used them, among other texts, to justify his elimination of the Old Testament (and most of the New!) from the canon. More subtle is the practice of contemporary church bodies that omit the imprecatory psalms from their hymnals. My own Lutheran tradition curiously omits the more strident examples from the pew edition while retaining them in the minister's edition. At the root of this uneasiness lies the clear witness of the New Testament, especially Jesus' challenge in the Sermon on the Mount, to love our enemies and pray for those who persecute us (Matt. 5:44; cf. 5:43–48; 18:21–22). Practicing what he preached, Jesus prayed for the forgiveness of those who nailed him to the cross (Luke 23:34). This critique becomes particularly acute in Nehemiah's case in that, not only did he not forgive his enemies, he prayed that they might not be forgiven by God. Without denying the truth of Christ's corrective or its authority for us, however, it must be emphasized that we cannot fairly apply that standard to Nehemiah.

Understood from Nehemiah's point of view, the prayer simply calls upon God, in language sanctioned by the conventions of the day, after extreme provocation, to deal justly with those who have aligned themselves against the divine purpose. The prayer thus provides yet another testimony to Nehemiah's seemingly unshakable confidence that he was pursuing God's will in the project.

This attempt to understand Nehemiah's position should not be taken as a warrant for such behavior in the Christian community. But that does not mean we cannot profitably use texts such as the imprecatory psalms and Nehemiah's vengeful response. Christians certainly are not unfamiliar with anger, rage, revenge, or violence, and knowing that they are unacceptable forms of Christian behavior does not make these feelings go away. By reading these violent words perhaps we will uncover our own deep-seated feelings of violence and stand accused of the same sin we so clearly see in Nehemiah. Then perhaps we will experience the message of grace and forgiveness in a new way for ourselves and consider sharing that expression of the gospel with others.

While Nehemiah's prayer is essentially an imprecatory psalm and consequently shares the interpretive difficulties of that category, the holy war posturing that dominates the second half of the chapter effectively minimizes the more objectionable aspects of that ideology (e.g., the absence of the climactic "ban," in which Israel was to eliminate the enemy along with any family or possessions that remained after the battle) in a way that accentuates the more positive contributions of the tradition. (For a perceptive look at the pastoral issues involved see the discussion of Joshua 6 in Fretheim, pp. 61–75.)

Two points require comment. First, in this text, as generally in the holy war traditions, all depends upon faith. This is seen not only in the exhortation to faithfulness that Nehemiah delivers (4:14) but also in the report of the limited nature of their human resources (vv. 10, 13) and the fact that they pray for God's help before they arm themselves (v. 9). What is required from the people is not strength of arms or superiority of numbers but a firm trust in the presence of God and the divine ability to deliver. The presence of the command, "Fear not!" in practically all the holy war narratives shows how crucial this aspect was. For Nehemiah to make use of the old traditions at this time was a stroke of genius; by reminding them that the cause was God's and that God would defend it, he effectively gave the demoralized workers the hope and courage they needed to see them through to the completion of their task.

Secondly, Nehemiah carefully avoided the temptation to

use the holy war traditions, with their emphasis on the power and efficacy of God, as a substitute for duty. Rather, he employed them to inspire and motivate the organization of the people. It is significant that the heart of the passage proclaims this double truth: God frustrated the plans of the enemy (v. 15), and Nehemiah established the so-called sword and trowel system that guaranteed the defense of the city (vv. 16–18). Both aspects, human and divine, are yoked together in the passage, calling to mind the famous dictum, "Pray as if all depended upon God, and work as if all depended upon you."

Nehemiah 6:1—7:3
Narrowing Reproach: Nehemiah

The obtrusive nature of chapter 5 has already been discussed in the introductory comments to the Nehemiah Memoir preceding chapters 1–2. Further comments on this passage will be found in conjunction with the discussion of 12:44—13:31 at the close of the commentary.

The final panel of the memoir (6:1—7:3) is loosely organized around five occurrences of the key word *(yr')* variously translated as "frighten," "be afraid," "intimidate," and "(God-) fearing" in 6:9, 14, 16, 19, 7:2 (cf. 6:13). Within this structure, two themes are woven together: the attempts to intimidate Nehemiah, as indicated by the repetition of the verb "to fear," and the final notices concerning the building of the walls.

   A   Building report, Sanballat and Geshem intrigue (6:1–9)
      B   Tobiah's intrigue (10–14)
         X   Building report, opposition (15–16)
      B'   Tobiah's intrigue (17–19)
   A'   Building report, securing the city (7:1–3)

Besides the occurrence of "fear" in 6:9 and 7:2, a word that appears near the end of each paragraph, thus revealing this section's general structure and coherence, the outer paragraphs (A, A') share references to building the wall (cf. X, v. 15) and setting up the doors (6:1; 7:1). This latter reference is important in that it establishes the period between the completion of the wall (6:1) and the placing of the doors (7:1) as the time frame

83

for this panel and argues for the inclusion of 7:1–3 in this section as the conclusion of the Nehemiah Memoir. It should also be noticed that the first paragraph (6:1–9) contains both thematic emphases of the passage in addition to mentioning the protagonists. It thus serves an introductory function for the panel as a whole.

The inner paragraphs (B, B') share references to Tobiah, either alone (vv. 17, 17, 19) or in emphatic position (vv. 12, 14), and they relate his two attempts to intimidate Nehemiah.

This leaves the statement that "the wall was finished on the twenty-fifth day of the month of Elul, in fifty-two days" (v. 15) and the characteristic notice of opposition, with its familiar introductory formula (v. 16), at the center of the passage.

The discussion of chapters 1 and 2 noted the importance of the term "reproach" (herpah: 1:3; 2:17). It was suggested at that time that the sorry condition of Jerusalem and the survivors, as depicted in the four destruction reports spanning the two chapters, was indeed a reproach against the God of the covenant who had returned the people to the land only to see them live in "trouble" and "disgrace," as the NRSV translates "herpah" in these verses. This reproach became the driving force behind the activity of chapters 1 and 2, with responses to the destruction reports by Nehemiah, Artaxerxes, and the Jewish leaders instrumental in the preparations for rebuilding the walls.

In chapters 3 and 4 the actual rebuilding of the wall is recounted amid the constant opposition of Sanballat and his associates. Once again "reproach" appears in a structurally significant position just before the crucial midpoint of the narrative: Nehemiah's plaintive petition that God might "Hear . . . for we are despised; turn their *taunt* back on their own heads . . ." (4:4).

In the present passage, however, the narrative has progressed to a point where the restoration of the wall is nearing completion. This advanced stage of Jerusalem's fortification compelled Sanballat and his cronies to change their tactics. No longer can they capitalize on the reproach of Jerusalem or the cadre of builders in their attempts to hinder the project. Now their attacks are aimed squarely at Nehemiah himself. Consistent with this change in tactics, we encounter the use of "reproach" here in a verbal form translated as part of a purpose clause by the NRSV, "in order to *taunt me*" (6:13). Whereas the object of reproach had been the sorry state of Jerusalem and the survivors in chapters 1 and 2, narrowed down to the builders in chapters 3 and 4, the object of reproach in 6:1—7:3 is Nehemiah himself.

In view of this structural analysis, the exposition will address in turn the three personal attacks on Nehemiah, then the building reports, and conclude with some comments on the theological implications they raise.

Three Schemes of Intimidation (6:1–9, 10–14, 17–19)

The three episodes of intimidation (6:1–9, 10–14, 17–19) are linked by the repetition of "to frighten us," "to make me afraid," or "to intimidate me," a rare form of the verb "to frighten," occurring in the last verse of each episode (vv. 9, 14, 19). In addition, the first two episodes share the expression "let us meet together" (vv. 2, 10) and a four-stage progression:

1. Occasion (1, 10a)
2. Scheme and Nehemiah's response (2–8, 10b–12)
3. Reason for scheme: intimidation (9a, 13)
4. Prayer (9b, 14)

The nature of 6:9b is disputed. The words "O God" are supplied by most translations to indicate that this is a prayer, though they do not occur in any manuscript. (For strong arguments against seeing 6:9b as petition see Williamson, *Ezra, Nehemiah,* p. 249; against this, however, must be balanced the structural similarity with 6:10–14, which concludes with an undisputed petition.) Thus, the primary difference between the two episodes lies in the double nature of the scheme (6:2, 4–7) and Nehemiah's double response (6:3, 8) in the initial episode.

The final episode (6:17–19) has more the character of a summary of the period more specifically described in verses 1–14 (cf. the vague description of the occasion "in those days," v. 17a). While the scheme can be said to be present in a general way in verses 17b–19a, and the reason for the scheme is clearly present in 19b, we hear nothing of Nehemiah's response and no prayer is offered. The letters that seek to defame Nehemiah contrast with the letters sent by Artaxerxes to vouch for Nehemiah at the beginning of his commission (2:9).

When we direct our attention to the various schemes perpetrated against Nehemiah, we see that they focus on three crucial themes of the book as a whole: Nehemiah's relationships with Artaxerxes, God, and the inhabitants of Jerusalem.

The first scheme (6:1–9), with its thinly veiled charge of sedition (v. 6), echoing the same charge *(mrd)* made by the same person (Geshem/Gashmu) in 2:19, strikes at Nehemiah's loyalty to the king. Throughout these chapters we have seen the positive relationship that existed between Nehemiah and Artaxerxes. Indeed, that relationship was utilized by God to set in motion the events that culminate in this chapter (2:8b). The lengths to which Sanballat and Geshem were prepared to go in their attack is disclosed in their attempt to discredit Nehemiah through false rumors of the resurgence of the latent political-messianic hopes of a century before, as proclaimed by Haggai (2:21–23) and Zechariah (3:8; 4:6–10; 6:10–14) with regard to Zerubbabel and Joshua. They surely were encouraged in this effort by the earlier success of Rehum and Shimshai with this same king (Ezra 4:8–16).

Therefore, Nehemiah's response (v. 8) is more than a flat denial. By accusing Sanballat and Geshem of trumping up the charge of sedition, he effectively calls their bluff, confident in his relationship with Artaxerxes and his correct assessment of the situation, namely, that the plotters were merely trying to intimidate the community in the hope that the resulting discouragement would cause the project to grind to a halt (cf. v. 9, "their hands will drop from the work, and it will not be done"). The urgency of the situation as well as Nehemiah's implicit trust are both underscored by the concluding prayer.

Though carefully structured in exactly the same way, the second scheme, this time devised by Tobiah and Sanballat to lure Nehemiah into disrepute through the hired prophecy of the otherwise unknown Shemaiah (6:10–14), is more subtle than the previous episode. In part, this subtlety is due to the presence of two rather opaque items in the text.

First of all, the obscure term "confined" (v. 10) remains enigmatic despite several attempts to decipher its significance as "unclean," "ill," "accused," or the like. One is tempted to suppose that, in accordance with the deceitful policy of Nehemiah's adversaries, Shemaiah misrepresented his seclusion as the outcome of some personal danger in an attempt to play upon the governor's compassion.

Second, the law clearly prescribes death for anyone besides the priests who comes near the altar (Num. 18:7). At first glance, therefore, it appears that the "sin" of verse 13 would refer to Nehemiah's illegal entry into the Temple as a layperson. But later in the narrative Nehemiah has no problem with entering those hallowed precincts to evict Tobiah and his belongings forcibly (13:8). The reading offered in the RSV margin, "And what man such as I would go into the temple *to save his life?*" (v. 11) suggests that the "sin" of verse 13 has more to do with the lack of faith Nehemiah would display by entering the Temple in order to secure his personal safety. This lack of faith would strike at the very heart of the trusting relationship with God that had contributed so enormously to the success of the project.

What is clear is that this subtle scheme strikes at the second of Nehemiah's thematic relationships: his loyalty to God. The success of the scheme depends on Shemaiah's ability to convince Nehemiah that he speaks for God, that he is in fact a prophet. No stone is left unturned in this regard. His "prophecy" is couched in poetic style, employs parallelism as well as rhetorical repetition, and displays a standard halting $(3 + 2, 3 + 2, 3)$ metrical organization usually found in the dirge *(qinah)*. Furthermore, despite its insidious nature, Shemaiah's proposal of Temple sanctuary from assassins may have sounded as plausible as it was pious to one in Nehemiah's situation.

Nevertheless, Nehemiah saw this clever charade for what it was: an attempt to discredit him in the eyes of God. Whatever the meaning of the enigmatic verse 11, Nehemiah's blunt reply indicates his recognition of Shemaiah as a false prophet, as does his narrative analysis of the situation in verses 12–13. Once again, the apparent ease with which Nehemiah discerns the true nature of Shemaiah's "prophecy" is indicative of the depth of his spiritual insight and reminds the reader that both Testaments urge us to "test the spirits to see whether they are from God; for many false prophets have gone out into the world" (I John 4:1; cf. Deut. 13:1–5; Jer. 23:9–32; Ezekiel 13).

The episode concludes with Nehemiah's short imprecatory prayer that God will "remember," that is "punish," Tobiah and Sanballat for their attacks. Readers might question these harsh words, especially in light of the more positive petition Nehemiah offered following the successful refutation of his opponents' first scheme (v. 9). But to emphasize the vindictive aspects of this prayer would be to miss the serious nature of this attack upon his relationship with God, an attack that contained elements of blasphemy. The presence of prophets, male and

87

female, dedicated to the destruction of the community within the nearly completed walls hinted that this continuing threat to the success of the restoration would not finally be removed with the completion of the city's refortification. Judgment was called for. In voicing his petition Nehemiah testifies to his belief in the appropriateness of justice and the necessity of response in the face of evil. This time, as in his imprecatory prayer in chapter 4, Nehemiah was content to deal with the present situation, leaving that final response to God.

The third scheme (6:17–19), as mentioned above, seems to provide continuing attempts to discredit Nehemiah at the time of verses 1–14 rather than a separate instance of intrigue. Nevertheless, the paragraph does indicate strained relations between Nehemiah and the nobles of the Jerusalem community, once again by means of letters. Thus, by the end of verse 19, the three areas of Nehemiah's concern—Artaxerxes, God, and the Jerusalem community—have all been touched upon in the context of intimidation designed to drive a wedge between the governor and his responsibilities. The "reproach" that would ensue would only benefit his adversaries. It is to Nehemiah's undying credit that he remained loyal to king and faithful to God throughout this exasperating period. That he will soon turn his undivided attention to the inhabitants of Jerusalem at least partially explains his lack of response in this passage and may offer some rationale for the present shape of the book as a whole.

The mention of what must have been mixed marriages in this context (v. 18) is also not to be overlooked. The continuing nature of this threat, which previously had absorbed so much of Ezra's time and energy, is here presented as a foreshadowing of Nehemiah's own grappling with this primary problem of the postexilic community. Each of the community's failures as recounted in chapter 13 (which, together with 12:44–47 and 5:1–19, comprises a "second memoir" with a different purpose than this material) is integrally related to the negative effects of foreign influence.

Building Reports (6:15–16, 7:1–3)

Though the building reports in this section serve the rather pedestrian function of providing the framework that supports the episodes of intimidation, the central paragraph (vv. 15–16) contains two additional items of special interest. First, the text, almost in passing, announces that the wall was completed on the twenty-fifth day of Elul (probably 2 October 445 B.C.). Despite recent archaeological investigations pointing to the low quality of the work in some sections, and the assumption that at least some of the earlier restorative work was intact, allowing Nehemiah to save time by relocating the eastern wall along the crest of the hill (cf. Williamson, *Ezra, Nehemiah,* p. 260), the reconstruction of the wall remains a remarkable achievement, especially so in light of the dispatch with which the project was carried out—a mere fifty-two days.

The second item of special interest in the central paragraph relates to the theme of opposition that we have followed through the course of the narrative and which culminates here. As noted earlier, there is a progression in these opposition notices. The adversaries become more numerous and geographically diverse until verse 16a: "And when *all* our enemies heard of it, *all* the nations *around us* were afraid and fell greatly in their own esteem." This note of reversal is amplified by the deliberate contrast between the first opposition notice, "it displeased them greatly that *someone* [i.e. "some *human,*" *'adam*] had come to seek the welfare of the people of Israel" (2:10), and the opposition notice of 6:16b, "for they perceived that this work had been accomplished with the help of *our God.*" Thus, that which had been clear to Nehemiah from the first stages of his mission (2:8), that which had inspired the inhabitants of Jerusalem to action (2:18), the divine intentionality with regard to the project, was now apparent to all those who had attempted to stand in the way.

A brief description of the security measures Nehemiah provided for the city is appended to the final building report in 7:1–3. The RSV margin rightly claims the Hebrew text is obscure at this point. In fact, as Clines remarks after a lengthy discussion of the problems involved, "With so many ambiguities it is remarkable that the gatekeepers knew what to do! All we can be sure of is that some unusual security precautions were to be taken" (*Ezra, Nehemiah, Esther,* p. 178). More significant is Nehemiah's appointment of Hanani to a position of authority in Jerusalem (the reference to "Hananiah" is probably explicative). Not only does this reference to "my brother Hanani," who first brought news of the destruction of Jerusalem in 1:2, provide an inclusion for the entire memoir, but the reasons for his

89

selection ("faithful" to the Persian king and "God-fearing," v. 2) sum up the qualities that Nehemiah has so consistently defended against all opposition, especially in this section.

THEOLOGICAL IMPLICATIONS

The complicated interweaving of attempts to intimidate Nehemiah on one hand with building reports that ultimately attest the success of his mission on the other suggests the theme of strength and security as a topic for theological reflection.

Sanballat and his cronies were right in perceiving that Nehemiah's strength derived from his conviction that he was employed in a work sanctioned by the king, authorized by God, and necessary for the continued existence of the community. From their perspective, these were the areas of support that needed to be dismantled. But their calculations went awry in their underestimation of the depth of Nehemiah's convictions and the extent to which he was able to draw upon them for strength.

In the confrontations Nehemiah experienced in this passage, readers are reminded that opposition to a "great work" (6:3) done for God can take many forms. The bullying threats of force that characterized the adversaries' previous attempts to thwart the project now gave way to deceit, innuendo, and personal attacks on Nehemiah and those relationships with king, God, and community that provided structure and meaning for his life. We can only marvel at Nehemiah's refusal to reply in kind. Whether his response consisted of blunt refusal to engage in debate designed to delay the operation (v. 3), explicit calling of Sanballat's bluff (v. 8), or determined rejection of any compromise of his faith in God for reasons of personal safety (v. 11), Nehemiah consistently dealt with the situation in an honest and forthright manner. No insincerity tainted his responses. No counterplots marred his approach. In this duel of diplomacy Nehemiah refused to play by the deceitful rules of his adversaries and countered their lies with open, frank statements that display his discernment of their traps and his refusal to be intimidated.

Throughout the passage, the repeated building reports remind the reader that in the midst of these final attempts to intimidate Nehemiah and upset the project, God remained faithful to the promise. Nehemiah never lost sight of that assurance, and soon his opponents would become painfully aware of the same in the poetic justice contained in verse 16 where, after all their repeated attempts at intimidation, they *"were afraid and fell greatly in their own esteem; for they perceived that this work* had been accomplished with the help of our God."

In the final analysis, it is this realization of God's continued faithfulness to the promise that will sustain the community, as it had Nehemiah, and as it does us. By recording the culmination of the wall-building project almost as an aside in the midst of the attempted reproach of Nehemiah, we are invited to entertain the thought that strength and security are not to be found in the fortifications of walls or military might but in the hands of God alone.

b—10:39

·l

the heart of the controversy surround-
ad Ezra–Nehemiah. A historical read-
y Ezra, who is clearly represented as
m to teach the Law (Ezra 7:10) and
, does not actually introduce it until
-building activity of Nehemiah some
. 8:1–8). This anomaly, together with
·e, has rightly led most commentators
pter originally followed either Ezra 8
tion of Ezra's reform, only to be dis-
of the Nehemiah Memoir (Nehemiah

trictly literary reading of the material
other sort. Nehemiah 7 ended with a
of Jerusalem's population and a "re-
o had returned with Zerubbabel. This
ed at this point, only to be picked up
e the plan for repopulating Jerusalem
e outlying population is brought forth.
inuity, at least, it seems to make more
hapters and proceed to the repopula-

istorical situation, it is clear that these
t from the surrounding context and
nother matter. Once again the narra-
rson, and Ezra, without introduction,
r in the drama, with Nehemiah rele-
rances (8:9; 10:1) and these only in a
ole. Since the final editor has decided
s way, we may set these issues aside
rative functions in its present setting.
ts overall narrative shape and then
il. Finally, some observations on the
es will be considered.

PART TWO

Renewal and Reform

NEHEMIAH 7:4—12:43

With Nehemiah 7:4 we begin the second major division of Ezra–Nehemiah. Part One had been structured around the three great returns and reconstruction projects that formed the salient theological moments of the restoration period in the eyes of the final redactor. With the temple, the community, and the city walls now in place, Part Two turns to the renewal and reform of the congregation. Again, as in Part One, three salient theological moments are singled out for examination:

1. The long list of returnees (Neh. 7:4–73a), already familiar from Ezra 2, is further interpreted in the context of renewal of the community
2. Nehemiah 7:73b—10:39, Ezra's so-called reading of the law, actually describes Ezra's renewal of the congregation's covenant relationship with God
3. The joyous dedication that caps Nehemiah 11:1—12:43 serves as the dramatic climax of the reforming work of Ezra and Nehemiah

If proclamation of the restoration community's continuity with the past has been a major goal of Part One, Part Two is concerned to extend those lines of continuity into the future. This accounts for the decided emphasis on renewal, reform, and repentance that punctuate these chapters.

Nehemiah 7:7[
Covenant Renew[

These chapters lie a[
ing the proper way to r[
ing must puzzle over w[
having come to Jerusal[
enforce it (Ezra 7:25–2[
after the arrival and wa[
thirteen years later (Ne[
other supporting eviden[
to conclude that this ch[
or Ezra 10 as a continu[
turbed by the insertion [
1—7) at a later date.

On the other hand, a [
runs into difficulties of a[
remark on the sparsenes[
run" of the list of those w[
narrative thread is dropp[
again in chapter 11, whe[
by means of a tithing of t[
In terms of narrative con[
sense to skip these three [
tion of the city.

Whatever the actual [
three chapters stand apa[
concern themselves with [
tive reverts to the third p[
becomes the primary act[
gated to two minor appe[
supportive, nonspeaking [
to present the story in th[
in order to ask how the na[
We will first investigate [
examine the story in det[
theological themes it evo[

NARRATIVE STRUCTURE

The narrative is presented in three scenes (7:73b—8:12; 8:13–18; 9:1—10:39) displaying an identical sequence. Each scene moves from time reference to assembly, to encounter with the Law, to application, and finally to response:

	Scene I *7:73b—8:12*	*Scene II* *8:13–18*	*Scene III* *9:1—10:39*
time reference	7:73b; 8:2	8:13a	9:1a
assembly	8:1	8:13b	9:1b–2
encounter with Law	8:3–6	8:13c	9:3
application	8:7–11	8:14–15	9:4–37
response	8:12	8:16–18	9:38—10:39

A number of repetitions further unify the three scenes:

1. Scenes one, two, and three:
   "gathered," "came together," "were assembled" (all *'asaph*, 8:1; 8:13; 9:1)
   reading from the Law (8:3, 8; 8:14, 18; 9:3)
2. Scenes one and two:
   "great rejoicing" (8:12; 8:17)
3. Scenes one and three:
   "understand(ing)" (8:2, 3, 7, 8, 12; 10:28)
   "Nehemiah the governor" (8:9; 10:1). Only here is reference made to the people "standing" (8:5; 9:2.; other uses of *'amad* mainly have the sense "appoint"
   six-hour length of service (8:3; 9:3)
   lists of officials and Levites (8:4b, 7; 9:4, 5)
4. Scenes two and three:
   "as it is written" (8:15; 10:35–37); only here in Nehemiah with reference to scripture
   "according to the ordinance" (8:18; 9:13, 29, 10:29)

We are thus meant to read the narrative as a whole, bearing in mind the basic movement of assembly—encounter with the law—application—response, as indicated in each of the three scenes. While there are some parallels in this movement to the synagogue service of later Judaism, we should not be tempted to read these parallels as somehow foreshadowing that liturgical tradition as has frequently been done. Rather, the movement

95

serves to unify the three chapters and emphasizes the importance of response to scripture.

In this light it is instructive to entertain the possibility that
these chapters have been assembled to portray a Covenant
Renewal (Williamson, *Ezra, Nehemiah,* pp. 275f.), with the
threefold structure: proclamation of the law (chap. 8); confession (chap. 9); renewal of commitment to the covenant with
general and specific stipulations (chap. 10), as seen elsewhere in
II Chronicles 15:1–18, Asa's reform; 29—31, Hezekiah's reform;
and 34:29—35:19, Josiah's reform (Kellermann, pp. 90–92). The
fact that these instances of covenant renewal all follow extensive cultic reforms, in material arising out of the postexilic situation, encourages this understanding.

Scene One: Joyous Renewal (7:73b—8:12)

This scene introduces the assembly—encounter with the
law—application—response progression that governs all three
scenes. While this paragraph is usually given the heading "Ezra
Reads the Law," the thrust of the text is decidedly not on Ezra's
reading of the scroll. This is clearly seen in the actions of the
people. First of all, it should be noticed that they "gathered
together into the square before the Water Gate" (v. 1); Ezra did
not summon them to this inaugural presentation. In fact, quite
the opposite is the case: *"They* told the scribe Ezra to bring the
book of the law of Moses" (v. 1). Secondly, the "wooden plat-
form" from which Ezra addressed the people is cryptically described, in Hebrew, as one "which *they* had made for the
purpose" (v. 4). In the syntax of the passage "they" can only
refer to the people described in the previous verse. There is
thus no hint of Ezra's imposing the law upon the people.
Rather, the people are portrayed as eager (v. 1), attentive (v. 3,
7b), and worshipful (v. 6b). Their solidarity is also emphasized.
The phrase "all the people" occurs no fewer than ten times in
this scene (vv. 1, 3, 5, 5, 5, 6, 9, 9, 11, 12), and the comprehensive
nature of the people is indicated by the repeated phrase "both
men and women and all who could hear with understanding"
(vv. 2, 3).

The Levites, the other significant group in the passage,
similarly take an active role in the proceedings of the day. Their
task is to interpret, explain, or possibly paraphrase in Aramaic,
the language of the people, what Ezra read in Hebrew, as an

96

aid to comprehension. This instructional activity of the Levites coupled with the text's progression and the pronounced emphasis on "understanding" (vv. 2, 3, 7, 8, 12) points to the response of the people as the main interest of the passage.

What a shock to the reader, therefore, when the people's response to the law, reverently read, painstakingly interpreted, and worshipfully received, issues in weeping (v. 9)! Not that grief over their laxity with regard to the law was inappropriate. Under similar circumstances in Josiah's time, their ancestors had also responded with mourning and weeping in repentance (II Kings 22:11, 19; II Chron. 34:19, 27). But this day, New Year's Day (Lev. 23:24), was "holy to the LORD" (vv. 9, 10, 11), set aside for another purpose, namely rejoicing and the blowing of trumpets (Lev. 23:24; Num. 29:1). Lest the reader miss this emphasis, the final verses of the text employ a narrative "double strike" to drive the lesson home. In parallel proclamations both Ezra and the Levites prohibit grief and enjoin rejoicing:

Ezra

a. this day is holy, do not mourn or weep (9)
  b. go your way, eat, drink, send portions (10a)
    c. for the joy of the LORD is your strength (10b)

Levites

a. this day is holy, do not be grieved (11)

People

  b. went their way to eat, drink, and send portions (12a)
    c. and to make great rejoicing (12b) *because* they had understood the words that were declared to them (12c)

This first scene, together with the next, thus functions as the first part of the covenant renewal that these chapters present: proclamation. The "joy of the LORD" (v. 10), freshly renewed through the teaching of Ezra and the Levites, will strengthen the people for the soul-searching that lies ahead in chapters 9 and 10.

Scene Two: Festive Renewal (8:13–18)

Many commentators prefer to see this scene as a simple continuation of 7:73b—8:12 on the basis of the time reference, "On the second day" (v. 13). In addition to the fivefold progression this scene shares with scenes one and three, the change in characters from Ezra, priests, Levites, and *all the people* to Ezra, priests, Levites, and *the heads of the ancestral houses of all the people* (v. 13) and the implied change in setting from the square before the Water Gate (8:1) argue for its autonomy. The narrative of this scene is lean. Very little material of an extraneous nature is found, and every word is necessary for the orderly progression of the passage. In fact the progression has been reduced to a skeleton compared with the initial presentation in 7:73b—8:12 and the greatly expanded version we will encounter in 9:1—10:39:

> time frame (13)
> > command "live in booths" (14)
> > > command "go out . . . bring branches . . . to make booths" (15)
> > > obedience "went out and brought them and made booths" (16)
> > obedience "lived in the booths" (17a)
> time frame (18)

Sandwiched between two time references that enclose scene two and inform us about the Feast of Booths (vv. 13, 18) is a naked description of command (vv. 14, 15) and obedience (vv. 16, 17a). As it stands, verse 15 has the effect of blending the encounter with the law and its application into a single concept that emphasizes the immediate response of the leaders to the injunctions of the law, so that Ackroyd may be right in slightly emending the text to read, "and when they heard this, they proclaimed . . ." (*I & II Chronicles, Ezra, Nehemiah,* p. 297).

In fact, the only extraneous material in this tightly structured paragraph is found in verse 17b, which functions as a rationale for the prompt action of Israel's leaders: "for from the days of Jeshua [a variant spelling of the more familiar "Joshua"] son of Nun to that day the people of Israel had not done so."

At first glance, this rationale is difficult to explain. The festival was celebrated both in Solomon's day (II Chron. 7:8ff.; 8:13) and in Hosea's time (Hos. 12:9), which are certainly after the time of Joshua. Even more disturbing is the mention of this festival in Ezra in the time of Zerubbabel (Ezra 3:4). What was so special about this particular celebration? The usual answer is that now the festival was being held at the centralized location of Jerusalem, but this is also true of Solomon's era, and it certainly was not true of Joshua. In light of the context's emphasis upon renewal, however, a more transparently theological motivation suggests itself.

A continuing theme in the narrative of these books has been the author's attempt to depict the events of the return and restoration as a "second exodus." Two elements in this paragraph serve to further that theme. First, the unusual phrase, "those who had returned from the captivity" (v. 17a), can be read as an allusion to the first "captivity" in Egypt. With the reader's perceptions thus heightened, the second element, the reference to Jeshua's celebration of Booths (v. 17b), is logically understood as a reintroduction of the interpretation of that celebration as a commemoration of the time Israel spent in the wilderness.

This is especially so since, according to Deuteronomic theology, Joshua's celebration is related in a context of covenant renewal (Deut. 31:9–13). Prior to Ezra's reinterpretation, this aspect seems to have been lost, and Booths was celebrated as a harvest festival in which God was praised for the bounty of the agricultural year. Now, after the reading and explanation of the law, the people were invited to focus on the festival's earlier emphasis: the effective presence and nurturing care of God toward the small community that had been so graciously redeemed and mercifully preserved. In this way attention is drawn away from the false security the completion of the walls may have engendered, as the people physically reenact their forebears' temporary dwelling in booths and reflect on their dependence on God for the seven days of the festival. As in the previous scene, the people assume a posture of "great rejoicing" (v. 17c), no doubt due to the recognition of the applicability of the earlier provisions of the law to their own situation.

This second scene thus serves as a graphic object lesson for the people. The law does have the power and ability to order

99

the fledgling community and can be depended on to provide the security and sense of continuity with the past they so desperately need.

Scene Three: Covenant Renewal (9:1—10:39)

This scene provides the climax to this section of Ezra–Nehemiah, which celebrates the completion of the walls. Joyous response to the reading and application of the law and festive response to the renewal of the community in its newly appropriated recognition of dependence on God had left the people in a joyful frame of mind. They are flushed with the experience that only the assurance of one's acceptability before God can provide.

This mood of joy will take on a more solemn cast here, however. The similarity of the restoration community to those who had been delivered in the first exodus was artfully drawn in scenes one and two. Just as that earlier pattern—hearing the law at Sinai and dwelling in booths in the wilderness—had culminated in a solemn covenant, so the present reenactment of the pattern will now conclude with a renewal of covenant pledges. The widespread difficulty of commentators with the text's expression of joy before penance and consequently their attempts to rearrange the text to provide the opposite order is thus seen to ignore the text's intention, as it now stands, to re-present the pattern of Israel's traditional story as that of the restoration community.

This is perhaps most clearly seen in the long confessional prayer offered by the Levites (the NRSV, following the Greek translation, mistakenly attributes the prayer to Ezra in v. 6) on behalf of the people in 9:5b–37, where the present community's solidarity with the sin of past generations is both stressed and acknowledged. This intentional identification also accounts for the pronounced sermonic feel the prayer evokes in the reader.

The most striking aspect of this last scene is the massive expansion of the fourth and fifth parts of the progression that unifies the three scenes. The greater part of chapter 9 (vv. 4–37) will be concerned with *application*, while all of chapter 10 (the Hebrew text rightly takes 9:38 as the first verse of the chapter) functions as the people's *response*. The emphasis on interpretation of scripture and appropriate response that we have seen throughout this section thus reaches its culmination in this scene.

Preparations (9:1–3)

These first three verses set the stage for the long expansion of the application and response that characterizes these chapters.

The scene opens with an indication of the setting: "the twenty-fourth day of this month" (v. 1), that is, the seventh month of Ezra's first year in Jerusalem. The ceremony thus provides an opportunity for the public expression of mourning and repentance so strongly felt by the people as they first heard the law read (8:9, 11).

The apparent contradiction contained in the notice that the same Levites who had rebuked the people for their earlier lament now led this service of mourning is troublesome for the reader. To what do we attribute this change in attitude? A careful comparison of chapters 8 and 9 reveals that the Levites are entirely consistent in their approach. The Levitical rebuke of the assembly's lament upon hearing the revelation of God's law in chapter 8 was justified from a theological perspective. Now, however, the recital of the people's own failure in the past forms the subject of chapter 9, a recital that properly leads to mourning and repentance, and that is encouraged by the Levites.

The sequence of joy followed by mourning, while initially jarring to our way of thinking, has strong liturgical precedent in the prescribed festivals of the seventh month. There, the joyous festival inaugurating the New Year is followed by the somber festival of Yom Kippur with its emphasis on repentance and concluded with the festive celebration of Booths (Lev. 23:23–44). In Christian liturgical practice a similar alternation appears in the juxtaposition of the joyous Advent-Christmas-Epiphany complex with the solemn Lenten season culminating in the joys of Easter.

Both aspects, joy and mourning, are part of our life before God. We rejoice in the sheer gift of God's gracious love freely given to us. We also tremble at the consciousness of our guilt in the eyes of this gracious benefactor and lament our feeble response. The alternating liturgical prescriptions of synagogue and church attempt to witness responsibly to the composite

101

nature of faith. The fact that contemporary congregations tend to emphasize the praise of Christmas and Easter at the expense of Lent's lamentation (the reverse of the problem Ezra encountered!) is a mark of our need to listen to the balanced counsel of the Levites.

The service itself is foreshadowed in verse 3. As in scene one (8:3), a six-hour service of scripture reading and confession is envisioned. In these brief verses the first three segments of the governing sequence, time reference—assembly—encounter with the Law, are concisely presented, thereby throwing the remaining final segments, application—response, into strong relief.

Application: Sermon-Prayer of Confession (9:4–37)

Ironically, the application of the people's encounter with what had been read begins with a confusing textual situation. Most opaque is the condition of the last half of verse 5 where the Levites summon the people to "bless the LORD your God from everlasting to everlasting." We may suppose that a line has been lost from the original (cf. Williamson, *Ezra, Nehemiah*, pp. 300, 303f.; and NEB), which possibly read:

> Stand up and bless the LORD your God:
> *Blessed are you, O LORD our God*
> from everlasting to everlasting.
> Blessed be your glorious name
> which is exalted above all blessing and praise.

As mentioned earlier, "And Ezra said" (v. 6a) is a gratuitous addition from the Septuagint. Thus, verses 5b–37 are the sermonic prayer of confession by which the Levites apply the earlier reading to the situation of the people. The prayer itself falls into an orderly, coherent structure:

A   Praise (5b)
   B   Confession in the form of historical retrospect (6–31)
     X   Petition (32)
   B'   Confession of present sin (33–35)
A'   Lament (36–37)

The movement from praise to lament that takes place in the outer brackets of the prayer (vv. 5b; 36–37) is unexpected. The usual movement in "psalms" of this type is quite the opposite.

102

Particularly in the laments, God works through his word to change our situation from lament to praise and restore the worshiper from a situation of despair to one of rejoicing. Westermann can even suggest that this transformation lies at the heart of Old Testament theology since Israel portrayed her experience of deliverance in terms strikingly reminiscent of this movement (pp. 20–21). Yet there is method to the madness of the text. The strong sermonic tone that will emerge later, as well as the contextual insistence that this is application, hints that the Levites' "prayer" is directed as much to the people as it is to God. If we are justified in seeing the covenant pledges that follow as the people's response, it could be maintained that they are the primary target.

The inner brackets (vv. 6–31; 33–35) consist in a long confession of sin, both past and present, that frames the sole petition of the prayer (v. 32). Here, the movement is from confession of past sin (vv. 6–31), by means of a historical retrospect that displays some affinity with other examples of this form (cf. Ps. 78, 105, 106, 135, 136), to confession that blends past with present sin (vv. 33–37) and emphasizes the community's solidarity with preexilic Israel.

The long historical retrospect of verses 6–31, though having an original setting in the postexilic cult (Williamson, *Ezra, Nehemiah,* pp. 309f.), has been artfully woven into the fabric of the covenant renewal depicted in chapters 8—10. Despite wide divergence among scholars on the elusive structure of this passage, the following scheme, based on the major periods of Israelite history, is offered as a way to organize the discussion:

1. Creation (6)
2. Abraham (7–8)
3. Exodus from Egypt (9–11)
4. Wilderness (12–21)
5. Israel in the land (22–31)

The first and last Hebrew words of the confession are "you" (*'attah,* vv. 6, 31). Thus, the personal nature of God is seen to span the historical retrospect, emphasizing the grace and mercy bestowed on Israel throughout this period. The Creator is depicted as Sovereign Lord of all creation: heaven, the heaven of heavens, with all its host, the earth and all that is on it, the seas and all that is in them (v. 6a) because God alone has

103

created them. More importantly, this Creator God preserves the divine handiwork (v. 6b), and the host of heaven appropriately responds with worship (v. 6c).

In pointed contrast to this worship, a very different response emerges in the sorry story of the monarchy (vv. 26–31), where Israel repeatedly disobeys (vv. 26a, 28a, 29b, 30b), is delivered into the hands of her enemies (vv. 27a, 28b, 30c), repents (vv. 27b, 28c), and is redeemed (vv. 27c, 28d), only to start the cycle of sin again in a pattern schematized at Judges 2:6—3:6. Despite Israel's rebellious response, the survey ends with the confession of God's grace and mercy in not forsaking them (v. 31).

The section dealing with Abraham (vv. 7–8) also introduces themes that are repeated later in the retrospect in a relationship of promise and fulfillment. The land is promised to Abraham in verse 8, and the promise is repeated in verse 15b. The fulfillment of the promise is foreshadowed in the gift of the boundary lands in verse 22 and is finally recounted in verses 23–25 when Abraham's descendants take possession of Canaan.

The exodus from Egypt (vv. 9–11) and the entrance into Canaan (v. 22) are presented as God's military defeat of Israel's enemies.

The wilderness section opens and closes with two narratives (vv. 12–15, 19–21) that are closely related by their joint references to God's guidance, nurture, and preservation through the pillar of cloud by day and the pillar of fire by night (vv. 12, 19) and the giving of the law (vv. 13–14, 20a), manna, and water (vv. 15, 20b).

The similarity of these wilderness narratives directs the reader's attention to the material they frame, verses 16–18, in which the dichotomy of Israel's rebellion in response to God's grace is emphasized. The reason for this emphasis will emerge after a closer investigation of these themes in the passage as a whole.

The first half of the confession (vv. 6–15) sings with one voice the glorious melody of God's gracious activity on Israel's behalf. Every verse of every section adds another demonstration of God's unmerited favor toward God's people. The Creator's purpose moves toward Abraham's election and issues in 104 a covenant that promises the gift of the land. The Promisemaker proves to be worthy of the name Deliverer as God redeems Israel from the bondage of slavery in Egypt, thereby

displaying divine commitment to the promise. But the Red
Sea opens into the wilderness, not the land of promise. Thus,
God's grace is seen in acts of nurture, guidance, and preservation as God leads the people forth toward the fulfillment of
the promise, all with nary a word of obligation. As if to emphasize this aspect, even the momentous giving of the Law on
Mount Sinai (vv. 13–14) is related out of chronological order as
one of God's gracious acts of provision. Throughout these
verses God is the sole subject of verbs that speak only of gift,
grace, and generosity.

With verses 16–18 the recitative of verses 6–15 extolling
God's grace moves into a duet in which Israel's rebellion, even
to the point of choosing a leader to lead them back to the
bondage of Egypt (vv. 16–17a, 18a), frames God's fidelity (v.
17b). God's response is couched in one of the classic Old Testament affirmations of divine faithfulness: "ready to forgive,
gracious and merciful, slow to anger and abounding in steadfast love, and you did not forsake them" (cf. Exod. 34:6; Num.
14:18; Joel 2:13; Jonah 4:2; Ps. 86:15; 103:8). These attributes
radiate out from this central affirmation in a cohesive network
throughout the prayer: "gracious" (v. 31), "merciful" (vv. 19,
27, 28, 31), "slow to anger" (v. 30, "Many years you were patient with them"), "steadfast love" (v. 32), "did not forsake
them" (vv. 19, 31).

Verses 19–25 return to the melody of unqualified grace as
God preserves Israel in the wilderness and fulfills his promise
of the land. All seems well as the people "ate, and were filled
and became fat, and delighted themselves in [God's] great
goodness" (v. 25b).

But the harmony of this section dissolves into the cyclical
cacophony of the next (vv. 26–31). The pattern of redemption,
so familiar from Exodus onward in the Old Testament—Israel's
cry of distress followed by God's hearing and deliverance—is
repeated in what strikes the reader as a parody of the faith it
was meant to evoke. The reader wonders at God's continual
return to his people despite their persistent rebellion. Will God
ever learn? Will they?

They will! The confession of verses 33–35 (B′) is a virtual
summary of the confession in verses 6–31 (B), as a sample listing
of verbal parallels indicates:

105

B		B'
8	you are righteous	33
8	Abraham and God faithful	33
6, 10, 17, 31	God does *('asah)*	33
18, 18, 24, 26, 28	people do *('asah)*	34, 34
26, 29, 29	your *torah*	34
16, 29	(not obey) your commandments	34
26, 29, 30	warn	34
17, 26, 28, 28, 29	turn, repent *(šub)*	35
22	kingdoms	35

The difference between the two confessions lies in the character of the second. Verse 33 sets the tone, "Yet you have been just in all that has come upon us, for you have dealt faithfully and we have acted wickedly." This "doxology of judgment," which publicly confesses that God is just even in the face of crisis brought by God and suffered by the confessor, shows that they *had* learned. The confession of solidarity with their forebears and lack of self-justification or excuse acknowledges that their present lamentable condition (vv. 36–37) is not due to any lack of care, concern, or faithfulness on God's part. Quite the contrary!

In this light, the placement of the prayer's only petition (v. 32) at the structural heart of the passage and framed by the two confessions is understandable. Introduced by "Now" *(we'attah),* as in the prayers of Chronicles and the postexilic correspondence (e.g., Ezra 4:14 in Aramaic), this burden of the message is an appeal for God to "not treat lightly all the hardship that has come upon us." Implicit in the prayer was the realization that God had not acted in a definitive way on Israel's behalf since the exile. Since the emphasis of the rest of the prayer is so firmly on God's continual grace, the people were led to expect an immanent manifestation of divine activity, especially now that they had recognized their own condition and need in this regard.

By means of this sermonic prayer, tailored to apply the previous reading to the contemporary situation, the Levites were able to motivate the people into making the proper response so woefully lacking in the historical survey.

Response: Faithful Covenant (9:38—10:39)

And respond they did. The transitional nature of Nehemiah 9:38, whether it should be included within the quotation marks that follow verse 37 or left as the introduction to chapter ten, is clearly indicated by the compiler's redactional phrase, "Because of all this."

An exceedingly simple structure organizes the response, which consists essentially of two lists: a list of those signing or agreeing to the pledge (9:38—10:29a) and a listing of the pledge's stipulations (10:29b–39). It displays a roughly chiastic arrangement:

a Declaration to make agreement (9:38a)
  b Leaders set their seal to the agreement (9:38b—10:27)
  b′ Rest of community joins leaders in agreement (10:28–29a)
a′ Stipulations of the agreement (10:29b–39)

Readers have long puzzled over the unusual ordering of verses 9:38b—10:27. The list of signatories (10:1b–27) employs the familiar ordering of priests (vv. 1b–8), Levites (vv. 9–13), and leaders of the people (vv. 14–27). But the heading (9:38b) reverses this order to "our princes, our Levites, and our priests." The discrepancy has been used to argue against the authenticity of the list, despite the necessity of some such list at this point in the narrative. A possible solution that takes seriously the present shape of the text arises out of the recognition of the transitional and redactional nature of 9:38b, as the following outline will make clear:

princes (9:38b)
  Levites (9:38b)
    priests (9:38b)
      Nehemiah the governor (10:1a)
    priests listed (10:1b–8)
  Levites listed (10:9–13)
chiefs of the people listed (10:14–27)

As this presentation makes clear, the material is not a haphazard construction, but carefully ordered with the three lists of signatories (10:1b–8, 9–13, 14–27) corresponding to their general introduction in the heading. One result of this structuring is that "Nehemiah the governor, the son of Hacaliah" is prominently presented at the center of the proceedings. This is most likely due to the compiler's intention to portray these chapters as the climax of the combined work of the two reformers.

In many ways the most significant aspect of this response is its curious character as indicated by the wording of 9:38a. The RSV rendering, "we make a *firm covenant*," while justified by the setting of covenant renewal and the presence of the formulaic covenant verb (*karat*, "cut, make a covenant"), obscures the linkage of the text's carefully chosen word for "covenant" (*'amanah*, "firm, faithful agreement"; cf. NRSV). Both with regard to Abraham (9:8) and God (9:33), the idea of *'amanah* ("faithfulness") has been decisive. It was Abraham's faithfulness that issued in God's covenantal promise of the gift of the land, just as it was God's faithfulness to that promise that motivated the gracious acts recited in 9:9–25. The "faithful agreement" of the people in chapter 10 is best seen, therefore, as a return to the faithfulness of Abraham and the covenant relationship that this return implied.

General (v. 29b) and specific (vv. 30–39) stipulations complete the covenant document. The general stipulation to which the people bind themselves is strongly Deuteronomic. "To walk in God's law" recalls Deuteronomy 8:6; "to observe and do all the commandments" repeats Deuteronomy 28:15. The pronounced Deuteronomic tone of the Law should not lead the reader into thinking that some form of the Deuteronomic code was the "law book" Ezra carried back with him and read to the people. Most scholars believe it was in fact the Pentateuch as we know it today.

The seriousness with which the people took this pledge is indicated by their entrance "into a curse and an oath" (v. 29a). Besides furthering the Deuteronomic coloring of the passage (cf. Deuteronomy 28 where this concept receives its classic Old Testament formulation), this phrase testifies in yet another way (cf. 9:33) to the people's recognition of God's justice in punishing covenant rebellion.

The specific stipulations can be grouped under three headings: (1) intermarriage (v. 30), (2) the Sabbath and the sabbatical year (v. 31), and (3) provision for the support of the temple and the clergy (vv. 32–39). D. J. A. Clines has clearly shown that these laws display an interpretive movement from the earlier situation toward an application to the setting of the postexilic community, especially in the area of the fostering of a national identity (*JSOT*).

1. The stipulation concerning intermarriage (10:30) re-

108

ceives pride of place as a testimony to the seriousness of this problem in the community (cf. Neh. 13:23–27). Here, while the basis of the stipulation is clearly Exodus 34:11–16 and Deuteronomy 7:1–4, its present formulation contains references to Ashdodites, Ammonites, and Moabites (13:23) in an attempt to update the earlier legislation.

2. Once again the close relationship between the Sabbath laws (10:31) and the events of Nehemiah 13:15–18 betrays the historical setting of this pledge. While all of the earlier legislation had promulgated rest on the Sabbath, in no instance do we see the buying of food defined as work as in these verses, directed to the present situation. The related stipulation regarding the sabbath year has no parallel in Nehemiah 13. It does, however, have reference to Nehemiah 5:1–13, which we have seen is closely related to that chapter in the Nehemiah Memoir.

3. The last sentence of the chapter aptly summarizes the obligations of verses 32–39: "We will not neglect the house of our God" (v. 39b). It also answers Nehemiah's plaintive question, "Why is the house of God forsaken?" (13:11, both verbs derive from *'azab*). Legislation concerning the temple tax (vv. 32–33), wood offering (v. 34), and first fruits, prime produce, and tithes (vv. 35–39a) is presented in ways that directly apply these earlier provisions to the life of the people.

Neglect of the law, which had issued in the disastrous consequences brought before the people in the Levitical prayer of the previous chapter, is seen, at least for the moment, to be the primary problem the new community faced. From the small beginnings the reading of the law prompted in chapter 8, the reader senses the gratification that Ezra would have felt upon witnessing the hearty response of the community to the law rightly interpreted and rigorously applied.

THEOLOGICAL IMPLICATIONS

We have seen that these three chapters have been forged into a unity from various materials of the postexilic period and ordered by the familiar theme of covenant renewal. With this theological motivation governing the intentional rearrangement of some of these materials, historical reconstructions are speculative at best, though this has not precluded a vigorous search for what actually took place. Taking the text as it stands, however, leads into a discussion of several theological themes of interest to the postexilic community as well as contemporary readers.

109

Perhaps Ezra's crowning achievement was the introduction of the law as the theological center of the community. Certainly, the later tradition's designation of Ezra as a second Moses derives from this fact. What arises in these chapters, however, is the serious attention paid to the process by which the written word functions authoritatively in the community. In all three scenes a liturgical reading of the law is followed by additional interpretation and application of the text to the lives of the people. Only when the people understand God's word as it condemns and consoles, do they respond in ever-increasing ways: first with a renewed sense of strength in the joy of the Lord, then with a renewed sense of their dependence upon God achieved through the reinterpretation of the Festival of Booths, and finally with a renewed commitment to the covenant relationship itself. The importance of the interpretive role of preacher and teacher in this process is thus lifted up and encouraged.

Closely related to this is the careful way in which the law is interpreted in chapter 10. Readers are familiar with the dichotomy between the letter and the spirit of the Law from the letters of Paul. Paul's hermeneutical principle of proposing adherence to the spirit of the law rather than the letter of the law is strongly foreshadowed in this chapter, especially when read in conjunction with the reforms Nehemiah brought to the community in chapter 13. As indicated in the previous section, in each of the specific stipulations, after the law has been publicly read, the intention of the original stipulation is made the basis for present application and response. The ability of scripture to speak to later situations is thus emphasized with a consequent growth in the authority of scripture, properly interpreted and applied, for the community.

The response of the people is another clear emphasis of these chapters. Two points may be made in this regard. First of all, though major movements in theological thought have tended to place the recognition of sin and its subsequent confession prior to forgiveness, other positions (most notably Augustine and Luther) have emphasized the inability of "the old Adam," or unregenerate humanity, to do this. Rather, it is only after the gracious activity of God upon the unregenerate heart that we come to realize our fallen nature and turn back to God in repentance and confession. Paul's classic description, coming at the close of his discussion of the power of the gospel to create our new status under God (Romans 1:16—5:21), "While we

were still weak, at the right time Christ died for the ungodly"
(Rom. 5:6), encapsulates this concept. This seems to be the case
in these chapters as well, especially chapters 9 and 10, where
the constant grace of God is depicted throughout Israel's history, and it is only upon their recognition of God's tireless return to them that the community is moved to respond in
covenant renewal.

Secondly, the tedious lists of signatories to the pledge that
conclude the renewal may be seen as one way of emphasizing
the *individual* response of those members of the community.
Coupled with these chapters' emphasis upon the communal
nature of the response, the reader is reminded of the importance of both corporate and personal assent as well as the responsibility that such assent requires.

Finally, mention should be made of the significance of
placing the reinterpreted account of the Festival of Booths
after the rebuilding of the walls and in the context of the covenant renewal. When the reader recalls that these books
opened with a celebration of this festival under Zerubbabel at
the first return (Ezra 3:4), it becomes clear that the whole period covered by these books has been presented as a unified
epoch of return, restoration, and rebuilding framed by two
celebrations of the ancient Festival of Booths in conformity
with what had been "written" and "according to the ordinance" (Ezra 3:4; Neh. 8:14, 18). This becomes yet one more
indication of the pervasive influence of Torah upon the life of
the reconstituted community.

Nehemiah 11:1—12:43
Joyous Dedication

The Tithing of God's People (11:1—12:26)

Once again the reader is confronted with lengthy lists! A
myriad of unresolvable problems with regard to the details of
these lists continues to baffle scholars. Obviously composite, the
lists display a long history of supplementation. Williamson is
probably correct in seeing them as later additions to the text at
some time following the combination of the materials that com-

prise the narrative of the reformers, Ezra and Nehemiah (Ezra 7ff.). Despite these difficulties with regard to details, however, it is possible to discern their general function in the narrative as a whole.

Throughout the exposition, it has been maintained that the appearance of these lists, so characteristic of Ezra–Nehemiah, serves a practical purpose, namely to provide a running commentary on the status of the community in relation to the developing situation of reform. The lists under consideration here are no exception. Nehemiah 11:3–36 ties the community, newly reconstituted under Ezra's reforms in accordance with the law, to the land, while Nehemiah 12:1–26, by recording the cultic personnel who have served the restoration community, links the contemporary cultic situation under Ezra and Nehemiah (Neh. 12:26) with the nascent situation that obtained at the time of Zerubbabel and Jeshua (Neh. 12:1).

Thus, chapter 11 begins where the narrative of the Nehemiah Memoir had left off, with the repopulation of the city (Neh. 7:4). It is crucial, however, that the placement of this material within Ezra–Nehemiah as a whole is taken seriously. If we consider it merely as the resumption of Nehemiah's reflections on his term of office, which had been interrupted by the intervening account of Ezra's covenant renewal, the repopulation will be seen as the continuation of his vision for the community. But Nehemiah neither speaks nor acts in this section. Technically, his first-person account resumes at 12:31 with the dedication of the walls. Reading the text as it stands, following Ezra's activity, the natural impression of the reader is that the *people themselves* (11:1–2), newly reconstituted under the law, rather than Nehemiah, are voluntarily responsible for the resettlement of Jerusalem as the firstfruits of their pledge not to "neglect the house of our God," as recorded in the last verse of the previous chapter.

The theological overtones in Nehemiah 11:1–2 are also not to be missed. In addition to the emphasis on the people's responsibility, which strengthens the impression that they have finally realized the seriousness of their situation before God and are now seeking to live within their covenantal obligations, verse 1 speaks of "casting lots" to determine who should make the move to the city. In our society such a procedure smacks of chance. But the Old Testament consistently presents this device as indicative of God's will. Proverbs 16:33 succinctly states:

"The lot is cast into the lap, but the decision is the LORD's alone," and this same theological assurance underlies such passages as the allocation of the Promised Land to the tribes of Israel (Josh. 14:2), the ransom of Jonathan (I Sam. 14:41–42), and the determination of Jonah as the cause of the storm (Jonah 1:7), among others. Also found in this verse is the theologically transparent "tithing" of the population whereby one in ten of the ordinary people would now live in Jerusalem.

Verse 2 adds the notice that the people "blessed" those who "willingly offered" to make the move. This borrowing of sacrificial vocabulary for the description of the repopulation of the city imparts a cultic nuance to the proceedings and continues the progression of sanctity that began with the reclamation of the altar and proceeded through the rebuilding of the temple and the walls to this inhabiting of what is now truly "the *holy* city" (vv. 1, 18). If von Rad is correct in seeing the dependence of the first part of this list on Joshua 15 (pp. 21–25), the geographical references to Hebron (the "Kiriath-arba" of 11:25) and Beersheba (11:30) are presented in such a way that the list recalls the extent of the kingdom in Josiah's time. This idealized picture of the community would thus extend the growth of holiness beyond the walls and the close environs of the city to Israel as a whole.

These considerations indicate that these lists have been strategically placed to inform the reader that the work of the reformers has been successful. The temple has been rebuilt and is fully staffed with cultic personnel. Similarly, the walls have been rebuilt and the city is fully inhabited with people purified and covenantally bound together under the proclamation and exhortation of the Law.

Joyous Dedication (12:27–43)

With the joyous dedication of the walls in Nehemiah 12:-27–43 the attentive reader senses that the narrative of the restoration has reached its dramatic climax. Verse 43 especially gives the impression that the story is here being summed up and recapitulated. The depiction of the celebration as a "dedication" *(hanukkah)* recalls the dedication of the temple in Ezra 6:17. The offering of many sacrifices also recalls the temple dedication as well as the reestablishment of the altar in Ezra 3:3–5. Then (Ezra 3:13), as now, the people's rejoicing

113

can be heard far away, though here, significantly, it is not mingled with weeping. The fivefold repetition of "joy" accentuates the unalloyed character of the festivities (12:43). In addition, it is God who gives men, women, and children cause for joy both here and at the reading of the law (Neh. 8:2–3). In a similar fashion, the procession around the newly restored walls of Jerusalem probably begins at the Valley Gate, as had Nehemiah's midnight inspection of those same walls in their ruined condition (Neh. 2:13). The sense of closure afforded by these recollections is striking and invites closer examination of this climactic passage.

NARRATIVE STRUCTURE

The structure of the passage has been disturbed by the final editor's additions to the Nehemiah Memoir. The lists of participants in verses 32–36 and 41–42 especially interrupt the narrative flow of the passage. By omitting these lists for the present, a coherent structure appears:

A   Preparations for joyous dedication (vv. 27–30)
  B   Two companies appointed (v. 31a)
    C   One goes to the right upon the wall (vv. 31b, 37)
    C'   One goes to the left upon the wall (vv. 38–39)
  B'   Two companies meet and stand at the house of God (v. 40)
A'   Performance of joyous dedication (v. 43)

This structure reveals the symmetrical ordering of the dedication as orchestrated by Nehemiah. After ritually purifying the clergy, people, gates, and even the walls, Nehemiah gathers them at the Valley Gate, opposite the Temple on the southwest wall, the point at which his initial circumambulation of the ruined walls began in chapter 2. His purpose is to impress upon the people the significance of their achievement by means of liturgy. By starting at this strategic location and processing in opposite directions on top of the wall, the two appointed companies reenact his earlier midnight investigation, arriving at the Temple for the dedication proper. One can only imagine the emotional impact of this procession, not only for Nehemiah, who would see it as a triumphant conclusion to his major task, but also for the builders, who had labored so courageously on this very structure. A further note of success is sounded when one recalls the scornful remarks of Sanballat and Tobiah:

114

> What are these feeble Jews doing? Will they restore things?
> Will they sacrifice? Will they finish it in a day? Will they revive
> the stones out of the heaps of rubbish—and burned ones at
> that? . . . That stone wall they are building—any fox going up
> on it would break it down! (Neh. 4:2b–3).

Indeed they will sacrifice! And what is more, the whole
company will process to the place of sacrifice upon the very wall
that could not support the weight of a fox! One need not apolo-
gize for the exuberant tone indicated by the framework of "joy"
that surrounds the passage (v. 27, five times in v. 43). This theme
of "joy" has appeared at other turning points in the narrative:
Ezra 3:12–13 at the laying of the foundations, Ezra 6:16 at the
dedication of the temple, and Nehemiah 8:12 as the people's
initial response to Ezra's reading of the law. Here, this theme
receives its final exposition.

Perhaps taking his cue from Nehemiah's liturgical symmetry, the final editor has enhanced this high point of the books
of Ezra–Nehemiah with his own embellishments. These too
display a remarkable symmetry, as the following structure
indicates:

First Company, processing to the right:
A Hoshaiah and half the princes of Judah (v. 32)
  B Seven priests with trumpets (vv. 33–35a)
    C Zechariah and eight Levitical instrumentalists (vv.
      35b–36a)
      X Ezra, the scribe (v. 36b)

Second Company, processing to the left:
A' Nehemiah and half the people/officials (vv. 38, 40)
  B' Seven priests with trumpets (v. 41)
    C' Jezrahaiah and eight Levitical singers (v. 42)

These additions to the memoir emphasize the cultic nature
of the dedication with their references to the priests and Levites who offered their musical skill to the proceedings in what
amounts to a "stereophonic" presentation with vocal music at
the front and instrumental music at the rear (Clines, *Ezra, Nehemiah, Esther*, p. 230).

The appearance of "the scribe Ezra" (v. 36b) is the primary
evidence for the contemporaneity of the two reformers. As the
relationship of Ezra to Nehemiah is the major historical problem of these books, much turns on the explanation of his pres-

115

ence in the text. Usually, it is seen to disturb the symmetry of the two companies, in that Hoshaiah, who parallels Nehemiah, is already at the head of the first company. This is regarded as evidence for the later expansion of the text and consequent denial of any overlap between the reformers. But the structure, as presented above, seems to place Ezra at the center of the literary presentation of the proceedings, with both companies framing his presence. In my opinion the reference to Ezra was added by whoever was responsible for the addition of the descriptive material that surrounds him, that is, the final editor of the book.

If this is correct, the historical linking of the reformers is indeed called into question. But the theological motivation is thereby set into greater relief. The text intends that the reader consider the contribution of *both* reformers in assessing the formation of the restoration community, especially at this climactic juncture where the triple concerns of the narrative as a whole—Temple, people, and walls—are symbolically joined at the convergence of the two groups on the walls outside the Temple.

THEOLOGICAL IMPLICATIONS

As we have seen, Ezra–Nehemiah presents the return from Babylon in three stages: an initial return under the leadership of Zerubbabel and Jeshua concerned with rebuilding the altar and temple (Ezra 1–6); a second return under Ezra concerned with rebuilding the people in conformity with the law, which entailed both negative (Ezra 7—10) and positive (Nehemiah 8—10) aspects; and finally the mission of Nehemiah, who sought to rebuild the walls of Jerusalem (Neh. 1—7:3). These three stages are linked by common themes. At each stage, God works through the Persian kings to inaugurate the three missions for the sake of Israel. In marked contrast to this benevolent activity, the people of the land seriously oppose the work of the restoration, whether that opposition derives from within the community, as in Ezra's case, or from the surrounding peoples. The overcoming of this opposition becomes a major task in all three periods. To these thematic links we may now add another, namely, the postponement or delay of the goal of each mission.

116

Just as Zerubbabel's goal of rebuilding the temple under the auspices of Cyrus was not realized until the reign of Darius, and

Ezra's mission of teaching and enforcing the law was dependent upon his public introduction of the law that did not take place until thirteen years after his arrival, so Nehemiah's task of rebuilding the city's fortifications, while speedily accomplished (Neh. 6:15), was not to be culminated until the joyous dedication related in these verses (Neh. 12:27–43).

The obvious question posed by the text as it now stands, therefore, is why the final editor has chosen to postpone the joyous dedication of the walls, which would most logically have taken place upon their completion, until after Ezra's reading of the law. One way of approaching this question is to take seriously the importance as well as the placement of the intervening material. When one approaches the material from this point of view, that the dedication service is intentionally delayed, a theological reason for the delay immediately suggests itself. Only now, after the covenant renewal that capped Ezra's task of reconstituting the people, and after the census and repopulating of the holy city, are the people (and the reader!) in a position to understand the full meaning and significance of the dedicatory service. This understanding of the service necessarily broadens its implications in that now it is to be seen as more than a dedication of just the walls. The temple, the city, and perhaps more significantly, the community that the walls circumscribe are also implicitly included.

This reading of the text invites the reader to ponder the church's long struggle with the subtle difference between sacred space and holy community. As a young pastor, I remember my embarrassment upon asking a colleague if I could "see his church," when he replied, "We haven't time. There are far too many parishioners for us to see them all!" The restoration of the church in our day has to do with the revitalization of the people of God. Ezra–Nehemiah will not allow us to separate the material aspects of our faith from the spiritual formation that allows us to see the holy purpose for which they have been set apart. The text compels us to see that the walls were not an end in and of themselves but rather the means to an end. By placing the dedicatory service at this point in the narrative, the editor emphasizes and maintains the proper relationship of walls as God's gift for security, and temple, Law, and faithful community as the heart and center of the life of faith.

A final theological implication concerns the nature of the dedication itself. The NRSV's decision to translate two distinct

117

Hebrew/Aramaic terms with the same English equivalent, "dedication," has added to the confusion at this point. One of these terms, *qdš*, has the meaning of "set apart for sacred use, consecrate, keep holy." It is used in contexts that speak of the cult, the priesthood, and functions that pertain to the sacred. Thus, Eliashib and the priests "consecrate" that portion of the wall for which they were responsible in the building report in Nehemiah 3:1. The other appearances of this term in Ezra–Nehemiah are found in Nehemiah 13:22 where Nehemiah commands the Levites to purify themselves and guard the gates in order to "keep the sabbath day holy," Nehemiah 12:47 where the Levitical and Aaronic portions of the tithe are "set apart," and a smattering of references to "holy," that is "consecrated," objects (Ezra 2:63; 8:28; 9:2, 8; Neh. 7:65; 9:14; 10:31[32], 33[34]; 11:1, 18). The other term, which appears in this passage, is derived from *hanak* and has a much broader meaning that is not confined to cultic matters. Thus, Deuteronomy speaks of "dedicating a house" (20:5), and Proverbs says "train up a child in the way he should go" (22:6), indicating a nuance of "initiation" for this term.

At first this distinction may seem trivial and hairsplitting due to the overlap in meaning these terms obviously share, but at least it prompts consideration of the dedication as an initiation, a new beginning for the people of God. This aspect of the text is especially important in light of the strong sense of closure that the dedication service also imparts to the reader, who is thereby asked to review the major themes that have engaged the text to this point. Without gainsaying the value of this perspective, it must also be urged that though the community has finally "arrived," it is also just beginning to function as a complete restoration of the people of God. That they can now joyfully celebrate the first phase of God's renewal, accomplished under God's gracious providence as Nehemiah recognized in his telling announcement "that this work had been accomplished with the help of [i.e. by the power of] our God" (Neh. 6:16), would hopefully empower the community to look forward and continue, with God's help, in the next phase of God's gracious plan to win back the world from the power of sin, death, and evil.

118 Again, it must be stressed that all that has occurred to this point and that is summed up in the joyous dedication is to be seen as a means and not as an end. The dominant note of the

passage is on what *God* has done. The people rejoice because
"*God* had given them great cause for rejoicing," as NEB translates verse 43. Herein lies the significance of the term chosen
to describe the companies that processed around the walls. The
Hebrew text refers to them simply but eloquently as "thanks-
givings" *(todoth)*. As is well known from the Psalms, Hebrew
does not distinguish between thanksgiving and praise. One
"thanks" God by "praising" God, and one "praises" God by
sharing with one and all what God has done. This nuance is
captured in my own tradition in the canticle that closes our
communion service:

> Thank the Lord and sing his praise; tell everyone what he has
> done. Let all who seek the Lord rejoice and proudly bear his
> name. He recalls his promises and leads his people forth in joy
> with shouts of thanksgiving. Alleluia. Alleluia (*Lutheran Book
> of Worship*, pp. 72f.).

Psalm 48, which has long been associated with this dedicatory
service, also sounds this note of proclamation as the goal of the
festivities:

> Walk about Zion, go round about her,
>   number her towers, consider well her ramparts,
>   go through her citadels; *that you may tell the next genera-
>   tion*
> that this is God, our God for ever and ever.
> He will be our guide for ever.
>
> (vv. 12–14)

Thus, these books of the postexilic period, so often maligned
as legalistic and dour, have as their high point a joyful proclamation of the redeeming work of God.

Remember Me, O My God

NEHEMIAH 12:44—13:31 (5:1–19)

That Ezra–Nehemiah reaches its narrative and theological climax with the joyful dedication of the walls recounted in Nehemiah 12:27–43 can hardly be denied. The gathering of loose threads, the echoes of prominent events in the previous narrative, the attempt to link the separate work of the two reformers, and the decided emphasis on the joy that permeated the celebration, all contribute to the unmistakable sense of closure readers familiar with contemporary novels experience at this point. It is therefore somewhat disconcerting that the narrative, seemingly oblivious to its own conclusion, marches on with nary a pause for thirty-five additional verses.

Among the various attempts to account for this additional material, the most common takes the closing verses of chapter 12, dealing with provision for the Temple services, together with the first three verses of chapter 13, dealing with the expulsion of foreigners, as an idealized picture of the community. Supposedly, this has been inserted by the editor (usually identified as "the Chronicler") to lessen the negative impact of the following episodes related in the resumption of Nehemiah's Memoir under the heading "Reforms of Nehemiah's Second Term as Governor," or the like.

It must be admitted that the confusing chronological notices of this concluding material give the initial impression of a rather haphazard anticlimax to the narrative and the above reconstruction has the merit of providing a possible explanation of the text as it stands. Nevertheless, when it is remembered that Ezra–Nehemiah consistently subordinates chronology to theology, a relatively coherent picture of this material as an appendix or coda emerges. Following an investigation of the literary clues leading to this conclusion, three observations on the theological implications they raise will be discussed.

Nehemiah 12:44—13:31
An Idealized Picture of the Community?

The generalizing nature of the chronological markers at the end of Nehemiah raises a number of difficulties for the reader. Does "on that day" (12:44; 13:1) refer to the day of joyous dedication (12:27–43), as seems most logical? This would provide chronological justification for seeing the events of 12:44—13:3 as an idealized completion of the dedication ceremony. If so, "now before this" (13:4) transports the reader back to a time before the dedication ceremony. But when? The text dates the occupation of the temple chambers by Tobiah in the period of Nehemiah's absence, beginning in the "thirty-second year of King Artaxerxes" (13:6), forcing an impossible delay of at least twelve years between the completion of the walls and their dedication. Clearly, "in those days" found in 13:15, 23, refers to the time of Nehemiah's later return, but this only further complicates an already hopelessly convoluted situation.

Hugh Williamson (*Ezra, Nehemiah,* pp. 380–384) has convincingly shown that 12:44—13:14 displays an overall unity of theme and should not be divided following 13:3. Throughout the section the use and abuse of the Temple chambers is at the center of the discussion. This is the case whether the specific point is (1) Nehemiah's forceful eviction of Tobiah, whose occupation of the temple chambers with Eliashib's support usurped their intended use as storehouses for the tithe of "grain, wine, and oil" (vv. 4–9), (2) his restoration of the usurped tithe of "grain, wine, and oil" that provided support for the Levites (vv. 10–12), or (3) his appointment of stewards in charge of the chambers (12:44–47; 13:11b–13). These close ties between 12: 44–47 and 13:10–13 concerning the appointment of stewards are matched by the equally close connection between 13:1–3

121

and 13:4–9 concerning the forbidden presence of an Ammonite (Tobiah) within the chambers. The connections suggest the following symmetrical arrangement:

A   Appointment of storeroom stewards for support of Temple personnel (12:44–47)
  B   Reàding of Mosaic law: No Ammonites to be found in the assembly (13:1–3)
  B′   Tobiah (the Ammonite) expelled from assembly in conformity with Mosaic law (13:4–9)
A′   Appointment of storeroom stewards for support of Temple personnel (13:10–13)

Seen in this setting, the troubling chronological references of 12:44 and 13:1 must be taken in the very general sense of "at that time" (cf. JB, TEV), pointing forward to 13:4–14 rather than backward to the day of dedication. As such, they cannot function as an "idealized picture of the community" designed to counter the rather negative portrayal in the rest of chapter 13. Furthermore, since the evil of Eliashib and Tobiah occurred while Nehemiah was away and not before the day of dedication, the equally troubling "Now before this" (*weliphne' mizzeh,* 13:4) must be interpreted *circumstantially,* that is, "in the face of this, despite this," and not temporally. Thus, *despite* the work of the reformers and the solemn pledge of the people that culminated in the joyous dedication of the walls, Eliashib, taking advantage of Nehemiah's twelve-year absence, dared to place Tobiah within the temple precincts. Upon Nehemiah's return, this breach of divine protocol was quickly and effectively terminated.

Nehemiah 5
A Second Memoir

Recognition of the emphasis upon Nehemiah's correction of temple abuses in verses 12:44—13:14 invites the reader to extend this line of interpretation through the remaining episodes of the chapter: Nehemiah's reform of holy space (12:44—13:14) is followed by his reform of holy time (13:15–22) and reform of the breakdown of the holy congregation through intermarriage (13:23–29). Besides the obvious parallel of Nehemiah's reforming activity, all three episodes are interconnected by the presence of foreign influence and share references to Nehemiah's rebuke (*rib*, NRSV "remonstrated" in 13:11, 17, and "contended" in 13:25) of the offenders. In addition, all three conclude with a stylized remembrance formula: "Remember me, O my God . . ." (13:14, 22, 31).

The tenuous nature of the placement of chapter 5 in the Nehemiah Memoir (1:1—7:3) has already been discussed. Here, it should be noted that chapter 5 displays the same parallels noted above: (1) Nehemiah's reforming activity (vv. 8–13), (2) the presence of foreign influence in the usurious practices of the wealthy (vv. 6–8), (3) his rebuke (*rib*, NRSV "I brought charges against . . .") of the offenders (v. 7), even (4) the stylized remembrance formula, "Remember [me], . . . O my God," used as a conclusion to the episode (v. 19).

While these parallels display the close connection of chapter 5 with the episodes of Nehemiah's reforms following his absence, three additional parallels with the first episode in this section (12:44—13:14) suggest that chapter 5 originally followed chapter 13 in the Nehemiah Memoir as a fourth episode framing 13:15–22 and 13:23–29. In verse 14 (cf. 13:6) we see the only other reference to Nehemiah's return to Babylon in the "thirty-second year of King Artaxerxes." Secondly, the mention of "grain, wine, and oil" in verse 11 echoes the double mention of these commodities in 13:5, 12. Finally, both episodes are concerned with Nehemiah's alleviation of economic distress in the community.

Within this framework of 12:44—13:14 and 5:1–19 the central episodes (13:15–22 and 13:23–29) display an identical structure, adding to the cohesiveness of these final verses as a whole:

1. Time reference "In those days . . ." (15a, 23a)
2. Description of problem "I saw . . ." (15a–16, 23a–24)
3. Rebuke "I remonstrated/contended (both *rib*) with . . ," making use of rhetorical questions and historical retrospects (17–18, 25–27)
4. Specific action (19–20, 28)
5. Threat (21, 29)
6. Statement of resolution (22a, 30–31a)
7. Remembrance formula "Remember me . . ." (22b, 31b)

This reconstruction has important consequences for the understanding of the nature and setting of the Nehemiah Memoir. While the presence of a first-person account ostensibly going back to the personal reflections of Nehemiah has been accepted by all, debate concerning the character of that account has continued to rage without consensus. Some scholars, noting the similarities between ancient Near Eastern inscriptions commemorating royal achievements, have sought to interpret the memoir as a report to the king concerning Nehemiah's accomplishments in Jerusalem. Others, noting the equally prominent similarities between Egyptian dedicatory temple inscriptions designed to recall the duties of senior officials, especially in connection with a remembrance formula, "Remember me, for good . . . ," have emphasized this aspect of the memoir.

The weighty form-critical arguments adduced from both sides have tended to offset each other, resulting in a scholarly stalemate regarding the character of the material. The major difficulty with seeing the memoir as a report to the king lies in its references to God in the remembrance formulae. The transposition of Nehemiah 5 (including the remembrance formula in verse 19) to the end of the work, and a division of the material, however, dissolves this tension.

1. A first memoir, the basic source of Nehemiah 1:1—4:23; 6:1—7:3, would then be a report to the king accounting for Nehemiah's activities regarding the building of the walls and the overcoming of opposition during his initial mission to Jerusalem. This would be similar to the ancient Near Eastern reports. Furthermore, the transposition of chapter 5 restores the dominant narrative progression in 1:1—7:3, in which every advance in the work is met by renewed opposition.

2. Nehemiah 12:44—13:31; 5:1–19, would then be based on a second memoir composed along the lines of the Egyptian inscriptions and indicating Nehemiah's later reforming activities following his absence, in which he asks God to remember him. (For a somewhat similar approach, at least with regard to 5:14–19, see Williamson, *Ezra, Nehemiah,* pp. xxiv-xxviii.)

Why the editor decided to move the concluding episode of this second memoir to a position following Nehemiah 4 is difficult to assess. Perhaps he thought the economic burden of the community, so poignantly portrayed in chapter 5, contributed to the impression of self-sacrifice and diligence evoked by the whole wall-building enterprise.

124   The editor's decision to conclude his work with the other three episodes of the community's relapse is more easily determined. According to widespread scholarly opinion, the commu-

nity's promise to abide by the covenantal stipulations in Nehemiah 10 *historically* took place following the events of Nehemiah 13 as a positive response to Nehemiah's reforms. By inverting this historical order, the editor refuses to relieve the tension between reform and subsequent relapse that has characterized the work as a whole. This refusal in turn forces the reader to contemplate this realistic, though not historical, understanding of the life of faith.

THEOLOGICAL IMPLICATIONS

The character of these concluding verses as an appendix or coda to the story of return, reconstruction, restoration, and reform provides the most significant basis for theological reflection. It is extremely important to notice that these books do not end on the optimistic note sounded by the joyous dedication of the walls in 12:27–43. Satisfying as that conclusion would be, it would utterly oppose a major theological theme of these books, namely, the community's constant temptation to abandon the covenants they had made and return to the evil practices previously corrected by the diligence of the reformers.

During Nehemiah's absence, each of the three areas of covenantal reform pledged in chapter 10—intermarriage (10:30), Sabbath observance (10:31), and support of the cult (10:32–39)—were carelessly disregarded as the community fell prey to the continuing temptation of foreign influence.

Readers of this register of the community's relapse may wonder how it could have occurred. Would they ever learn? Or had the patient teaching of Ezra and the tireless work of Nehemiah been in vain? How could the religious leaders of the community be at the vanguard of this apostasy? But there is little cause for wonder. Scripture is saturated with stories testifying to this basic human weakness. Israel's worship of the golden calf (Exodus 32) during Moses' absence following the covenant on Mount Sinai is only the most extreme example that could be cited from the Old Testament. The New Testament also recognizes this all-too-human propensity for backsliding and never tires of graphicallʏ portraying its effect on the behavior of even the most committed. Of Jesus' twelve disciples one turned out to be a thief who stole from their common purse and handed Jesus over to the authorities. Peter, his favorite, who had claimed to have left everything to follow him (Mark 10:28), denied Jesus three times out of concern for his own safety.

125

Despite Jesus' warnings about selfishness and his demands that they take the last place and seek to serve, James and John vie for positions of authority in the kingdom (Mark 10).

The text, as it has been presented, reminds all readers of the continuing need for commitment and challenges them to seek out those areas in their lives that call for reform and renewal.

This call to commitment becomes all the more pressing in the light of a striking feature of the text. Throughout the previous narrative each major section has explicitly attributed the success of return, reconstruction, reform, and renewal to the gracious activity of God. No such statement appears here, and the reader is confronted with the distinct possibility that this time the community has gone too far, that the dire warnings of Ezra regarding the tenuous character of their situation were all too perceptive. Their lapse during Nehemiah's absence was a testimony to the positive influence his presence and example had inspired, and to what is likely to happen to the community when he is gone. The text leaves the reader wondering if the community will ever be able to function apart from the inspired leadership of individuals such as Ezra and Nehemiah. One may even wonder if Nehemiah's personal prayers for remembrance, which punctuate the various episodes of his courageous labors against the collapse of the community, were his own cries for divine assurance. If so, we can only marvel at the depth of his personal faith and commitment in the face of God's perceived absence.

Sobering as this word may be, we are not meant to dwell on this pessimistic portrayal of the community. Their failure is, after all, only an example of the sin that pervades the human race and the reason that all attempts at a lasting restoration of communion with God based on the law are doomed to failure. The restoration of Jerusalem with its temple and walls was not the final fulfillment of the prophetic hope. The walls would not withstand subsequent attack, and the temple itself would later be destroyed. But from the loins of that sinful community something new would appear, not merely a restoration of the old but a new departure, a totally new avenue of approach in which God himself in the life, death, and resurrection of Jesus Christ would fulfill the demands of the law where Israel could not. It is to this final fulfillment of the prophetic hope that Ezra–Nehemiah ultimately points.

BIBLIOGRAPHY

1. For further study

ACKROYD, PETER R. *Exile and Restoration; A Study of Hebrew Thought of the Sixth Century B.C.* OLD TESTAMENT LIBRARY (Philadelphia: Westminster Press, 1968).
————. *I & II Chronicles, Ezra, Nehemiah.* TORCH BIBLE COMMENTARIES (London: SCM Press, 1973).
ALTER, ROBERT. *The Art of Biblical Narrative* (New York: Basic Books, 1981).
BLENKINSOPP, JOSEPH. *Ezra–Nehemiah.* OLD TESTAMENT LIBRARY (Philadelphia: Westminster Press, 1988).
CLINES, D. J. A. *Ezra, Nehemiah, Esther.* NEW CENTURY BIBLE (Grand Rapids: Wm. B. Eerdmans Publishing Co., 1984).
KIDNER, DEREK. *Ezra and Nehemiah.* TYNDALE OLD TESTAMENT COMMENTARIES (Downers Grove, Ill.: InterVarsity Press, 1979).
McCONVILLE, J. G. *Ezra, Nehemiah and Esther.* DAILY STUDY BIBLE (Philadelphia: Westminster Press, 1985).
MICHAELI, F. *Les livres des Chroniques, d'Esdras et de Néhémie.* COMMENTAIRE DE L'ANCIEN TESTAMENT XVI (Neuchâtel: Delachaux & Niestlé, 1967).
THRONTVEIT, M. "Linguistic Analysis and the Question of Authorship in Chronicles, Ezra, and Nehemiah." *Vetus Testamentum* 32:201–216 (1982).
WILLIAMSON, H. G. M. *Ezra, Nehemiah.* WORD BIBLICAL COMMENTARY (Waco, Tex.: Word Books, 1985).

2. Literature cited

ACKROYD, PETER R. *I & II Chronicles, Ezra, Nehemiah.* TORCH BIBLE COMMENTARIES (London: SCM Press, 1973).
BICKERMAN, E. J. "En marge de l'Écriture. I.—Le comput des années de règne des Achéménides (Néh., i, 2; ii, 1 et Thuc., viii, 58." *Revue Biblique* 88:19–23 (1981).
BLENKINSOPP, JOSEPH. *Ezra–Nehemiah.* OLD TESTAMENT LIBRARY (Philadelphia: Westminster Press, 1988).
BOECKER, H. J. *Redeformen des Rechtsleben im Alten Testament.* WISSENSCHAFTLICHE MONOGRAPHIEN ZUM ALTEN

UND NEUEN TESTAMENT 14 (Neukirchen-Vluyn: Neukirchener Verlag, 1964).

BOSSMAN, D. "Ezra's Marriage Reform: Israel Redefined." *Biblical Theology Bulletin* 9:32–38 (1979).

BRUEGGEMANN, W. *The Message of the Psalms: A Theological Commentary* (Minneapolis: Augsburg, 1984).

CARMODY, J., D. L. CARMODY, and R. L. COHN. *Exploring the Hebrew Bible* (Englewood Cliffs, N.J.: Prentice-Hall, 1988).

CLINES, D. J. A. *Ezra, Nehemiah, Esther.* NEW CENTURY BIBLE (Grand Rapids: Wm. B. Eerdmans Publishing Co., 1984).

———. "Nehemiah 10 as an Example of Early Jewish Biblical Exegesis." *Journal for the Study of the Old Testament* 21:-111–117 (1981).

COGGINS, R. J. *The Books of Ezra and Nehemiah.* THE CAMBRIDGE BIBLE COMMENTARY (Cambridge: Cambridge University Press, 1976).

FRETHEIM, TERENCE E. *Deuteronomic History* (Nashville: Abingdon Press, 1983).

GUNNEWEG, A. H. J. "Zur Interpretation der Bücher Esra–Nehemiah." CONGRESS VOLUME, VIENNA. 1980. *Vetus Testamentum,* Supplement 32:146–161 (1981).

———. *Esra.* KOMMENTAR ZUM ALTEN TESTAMENT XIXi (Gütersloh: Gütersloher Verlagshaus Gerd Mohn, 1985).

JAPHET, SARAH. "The Supposed Common Authorship of Chronicles and Ezra-Nehemiah Investigated Anew." VETUS TESTAMENTUM 18:330–371 (1968).

KELLERMANN, U. *Nehemia: Quellen, Überlieferung und Geschichte.* BEIHEFTE ZUR ZEITSCHRIFT FÜR DIE ALTTESTAMENTLICHE WISSENSCHAFT 102 (Berlin: Töpelmann, 1967).

KIDNER, DEREK. *Ezra and Nehemiah.* TYNDALE OLD TESTAMENT COMMENTARIES (Downers Grove, Ill.: InterVarsity Press, 1979).

KOCH, KLAUS. "Ezra and the Origins of Judaism." *Journal of Semitic Studies* 19:173–197 (1974).

LEWIS, C. S. *Reflections on the Psalms* (New York: Harcourt, Brace & Co., 1958).

LUTHERAN BOOK OF WORSHIP (Minneapolis: Augsburg, 1978).

McCONVILLE, J. G. *Ezra, Nehemiah and Esther.* DAILY STUDY BIBLE (Philadelphia: Westminster Press, 1985).

———. *I & II Chronicles.* DAILY STUDY BIBLE (Philadelphia: Westminster Press, 1984).

MICHAELI, F. *Les livres des Chroniques, d'Esdras et de Néhémie.* COMMENTAIRE DE L'ANCIEN TESTAMENT XVI (Neuchâtel: Delachaux & Niestlé, 1967).

MILGROM, JACOB. *Numbers.* THE JPS TORAH COMMENTARY (Philadelphia: Jewish Publication Society, 1990).

MOWINCKEL, S. *Studien zu dem Buche Ezra–Nehemia I: Die nachchronistische Redaktion des Buches. Die Listen.* SKRIFTER UTGITT AV DET NORSKE VIDENSKAPS AKADEMI I OSLO (Oslo: Universitetsforlaget, 1964).

RUDOLPH, W. *Ezra und Nehemia.* HANDBUCH ZUM ALTEN TESTAMENT 20 (Tübingen: Mohr, 1949).

TALMON, S. "Ezra and Nehemiah (Books and Men)." *Interpreter's Dictionary of the Bible* Supplementary Volume (New York: Abingdon Press, 1976): 317–328.

THRONTVEIT, M. "Linguistic Analysis and the Question of Authorship in Chronicles, Ezra, and Nehemiah." *Vetus Testamentum* 32:201–216 (1982).

VON RAD, GERHARD. *Das Geschichtsbild des chronistischen Werkes.* BEITRÄGE ZUR WISSENSCHAFT VOM ALTEN UND NEUEN TESTAMENT 4/3 (Stuttgart: W. Kohlhammer, 1930).

WESTERMANN, CLAUS. "The Role of the Lament in the Theology of the Old Testament." *Interpretation* 28:20–38 (1974).

WILLIAMSON, H. G. M. *Ezra, Nehemia.* WORD BIBLICAL COMMENTARY (Waco, Tex.: Word Books, 1985).

———. "The Composition of Ezra i–vi." *Journal of Theological Studies* 34:1–30 (1983).

———. "Nehemiah's Wall Revisited." *Palestine Exploration Quarterly* 116:81–88 (1984).